Ogling Ladies

UNIVERSITY PRESS OF FLORIDA

Florida A&M University, Tallahassee
Florida Atlantic University, Boca Raton
Florida Gulf Coast University, Ft. Myers
Florida International University, Miami
Florida State University, Tallahassee
New College of Florida, Sarasota
University of Central Florida, Orlando
University of Florida, Gainesville
University of North Florida, Jacksonville
University of South Florida, Tampa
University of West Florida, Pensacola

Ogling Ladies

SCOPOPHILIA IN MEDIEVAL GERMAN LITERATURE

Sandra Lindemann Summers

University Press of Florida

Gainesville/Tallahassee/Tampa/Boca Raton
Pensacola/Orlando/Miami/Jacksonville/Ft. Myers/Sarasota

The publication of this book is made possible in part by a grant from the Department
of German and Slavic Languages at the University of North Carolina at Chapel Hill.

All images reproduced courtesy of the University of Heidelberg Library.

This book may be available in an electronic edition.

First cloth printing, 2013
First paperback printing, 2019

24 23 22 21 20 19   6 5 4 3 2 1

Library of Congress Cataloging-in-Publication Data
Summers, Sandra Lindemann, 1963–
Ogling ladies : scopophilia in medieval German literature / Sandra Lindemann Summers.
p. cm.
Includes bibliographical references and index.
Summary: An analysis of medieval literature through an exploration of the female gaze.
ISBN 978-0-8130-4418-7 (cloth : alk. paper)
ISBN 978-0-8130-6421-5 (pbk.)
1. German literature—Middle High German, 1050–1500—History and criticism.
2. Voyeurism in literature. 3. Women in literature. 4. Gaze in literature. I. Title.
PT179.S96 2013
830.9'3538—dc23   2012046696

The University Press of Florida is the scholarly publishing agency for the State University
System of Florida, comprising Florida A&M University, Florida Atlantic University, Florida
Gulf Coast University, Florida International University, Florida State University, New College
of Florida, University of Central Florida, University of Florida, University of North Florida,
University of South Florida, and University of West Florida.

University Press of Florida
2046 NE Waldo Road
Suite 2100
Gainesville, FL 32609
http://upress.ufl.edu

To my mother, Doris Lindemann

Contents

List of Illustrations viii

Preface ix

Acknowledgments xi

Introduction 1

1. "A lady should never look directly at a male visitor":
Thomasin von Zerclaere 11

2. "Wild glances": *Winsbeckin* and *Der Renner* 21

3. "The woman behind the wall":
Heinrich von Melk and Der Stricker 35

4. "He was as handsome as he could be!": Male Beauty
and the Ogling Lady in the *Eneasroman* 47

5. "The most handsome knight that ever lived":
Female Scopophilia in *Parzival* 68

6. "Lady, you saw it with your own eyes!": Enite and the Perfect
Female Gaze in Hartmann's *Erec* 88

7. Knight or Eye Candy? The Gendering Gaze
in Hartmann von Aue's *Iwein* 105

Conclusion 122

Appendix: English translations of Heinrich von Melk's *Von des todes
gehugde* and Der Stricker's *Die eingemauerte Frau* 127

Notes 153

Bibliography 157

Index 173

Illustrations

1. fol. 11v "Herzog Heinrich von Breslau" 63
2. fol. 17r "Der Herzog von Anhalt" 64
3. fol. 43v "Graf Wernher von Homberg" 65
4. fol. 46v "Herr Jakob von Warte" 66
5. fol. 52r "Herr Walther von Klingen" 67

Preface

An ogling woman featured in a recent television commercial: A mechanic in tight jeans is bending over a car engine while a woman standing across the street stares at his behind. In the next scene, the same woman appears in her living room with her husband, a balding, middle-aged man. She hands him a shopping bag containing the same jeans worn by the mechanic. She impatiently and breathlessly demands: "Put these on. Now." I conducted an unscientific poll among friends and found that both male and female viewers of the commercial thought it funny. But what if the gender roles were reversed? What if the ogling character were a husband who surprises his wife with a skirt he had seen on a more attractive woman? Such a commercial does not exist, because it would be offensive and, more importantly, it wouldn't sell the product. Simply put, people perceive the male gaze and the female gaze as two entirely different things.

Gazing female characters caught my eye when I translated Hartmann von Aue's *Iwein* from Middle High German into English. Especially surprising was a passage describing a young girl in the act of ogling the naked, unconscious knight Iwein. I had previously assumed that the courtly lady and not the knight would be the object of the gaze. I became curious about the gender dynamics between the characters and wanted to know more. Were there other scenes where women ogled men, where male characters, knowingly or unknowingly, became scopophilic objects of the female gaze? The answer is a resounding yes. Medieval texts are inhabited by a host of females taking pleasure in ogling male bodies.

It is my belief that this exploration of the medieval female gaze transcends medieval scholarship; it affects our understanding of the broader problematic of gender perceptions and social structuring in Western civilization. My goal as a feminist medievalist is to use medieval texts to illuminate and lay bare structures of patriarchy, documenting how they were implemented, how they worked, and why. By reading the medieval cultural artifacts through a psychoanalytic lens—a strategy I explain in the introduction to this book—I will show that the representation of the female gaze is broadly split into an approved/approving motherly gaze and an undesirable critical/sexual gaze. Guiding and containing the female gaze through normative and prescriptive writing formed a complex and sometimes contradictory substructure of medieval patriarchy where women had limited agency and were traded as exchange objects.

Acknowledgments

I warmly thank Ann Marie Rasmussen, who is the main reason why I fell in love with medieval German literature. Her input and support were essential to this project from its inception to its completion. I would like to acknowledge the University Library of Heidelberg, where I was generously granted access to rare medieval manuscripts and received permission to reprint the wonderful Manesse miniatures. I thank my acquiring editor at University Press of Florida, Amy Gorelick, for her creative input and, of course, for selecting this book for publication. Jonathan Lawrence deserves special thanks for his meticulous work in editing the manuscript for publication. I sincerely thank the chair of the Department of Germanic and Slavic Languages at the University of North Carolina–Chapel Hill, Clayton Koelb, for supporting this project. The friendship of Halcyon Rigdon sustained me during the editorial process. Last, I owe gratitude to my husband, Thomas Stran Summers, and my daughter, Berta Jane Summers, for proofreading the original manuscript, and to my son, Erik Stran Summers, for discussing ideas on long walks with our dog Max.

Introduction

In the European Middle Ages, people did not perceive looking as a harm-
less, passive pastime. To the contrary, the harm that a person's gaze could
cause was greatly feared; a stare was understood as an act of aggression. To
be clear, the notion of the gaze as a destructive force predates medieval texts.
Beautiful Narcissus, for instance, tragically loses his life because his eyes
remain fixed on his own reflection for too long. Orpheus cannot control
himself and defies the gods' command not to look at his beloved Eurydice
in Hades, losing her forever. Yet the most poignant Greek mythological
example of the destructive power of the gaze is the Gorgon Medusa, who
kills onlookers through a redoubled death stare. Her own dead eyes look
at the mortified gazer; the twin horrors of being seen by the Gorgon while
beholding her horrific severed head turn the victim to stone.[1] Plato, in his
physics of vision, imagined that rays of light projected from the eyes like
darts. Other ancient philosophers developed theories of eye emanations or
extromissions. Theophrastus, a student of Plato and Aristotle, taught that
eyes contained hidden fire which flashed out when a warrior died in battle. This system of ideas was further developed by Galen, Euclid, Al-Kindi,
Roger Bacon, and John Pecham before eventually falling out of favor in early
modern Europe.[2]

Beginning in antiquity, spanning medieval and early modern times, people, especially women, who stared openly and directly at others ran the risk
of being accused of casting the evil eye. The evil-eye belief, found in many
parts of the world, is the superstition that looking at someone or something
can cause injury and damage; it is conceptually and linguistically linked
to envy, which is the suffering felt over another person's good fortune. The

envy-afflicted person engages in desiring and aggressive staring, thereby dominating and harming the object of the gaze.[3]

The word "eye" itself, as well as the German word "Auge," both derive from the Germanic word "augon," which was not a neutral notion; negative connotations survive in the related lexemes "ferocious" and "atrocious" (Ayto 42). The Latin verb "invidere"—in-videre, to look deeply into—is translated as "durch den bösen Blick Unheil bringen" (Menge 294). The noun "invidia" means malice, envy, jealousy, hatred, bitterness. Even if most people today wouldn't give much credence to sayings like "looks can kill," fragmentary evidence of the superstition survives in expressions like "burning holes in the back of someone's head." Etymological remnants of both the evil-eye belief and the extromission theory are found in the modern German language, in idioms such as "mit Blicken durchbohren," "Blicke schiessen," "mit den Blicken/Augen verschlingen," and "die Augen sprühen Funken/Blitze."[4] Believers were convinced that enviously looking at someone or something, ogling a coveted object, person, or animal, was an act of aggression.[5] Destitute women, barren women, old women, widows, and women with unusual physical features were thought to have an especially devastating gaze (Chevalier and Gheerbrant 365). Jehan Le Fèvre, a late medieval cleric, found it necessary to warn husbands of their wives' malevolent stare: "I tell you truly . . . she is like a basilisk and may God protect you from this snake that kills people with its gaze" (qtd. in Blamires 183).

Becoming the victim of someone's malevolent stare was quite serious. Alan Dundes lists the most common symptoms: loss of appetite, excessive yawning, hiccoughs, vomiting, fever, loss of sexual potency, and death (*Evil Eye* 290). Protective countermeasures against this danger are abundant and varied; the veiling of women in the Muslim world, for example, is one of the many preventative devices. The tilak, the forehead dot worn by many Hindu women, repels envious glances. In Mediterranean countries, the wearing of charms, beads, and amulets shaped like an eye symbolically returns and reflects the malevolent stare.[6]

An ancient way of counteracting the threat of the evil eye, art-historical evidence suggests, is to defecate upon it. One sculpture recently unearthed at Pompeii represents a man in a defecating position next to a woman. Above the image of the squatting man is the inscription "Cacator cave malum." Another sculpture renders a figure with bare buttocks sitting on a giant eye. Folkloric evidence indicates that feces were thought to have protective powers; there is, for example, an ancient Scottish custom of putting dung in a newborn calf's mouth as a safeguard against the evil eye (Dundes, *Evil Eye* 11).

During the late medieval and early modern periods, countermeasures against the evil eye moved beyond the protective wearing of talismans or amulets to more drastic action: hundreds of women (and a few men) were burned as witches for the sole reason of having been suspected and convicted of casting the evil eye.

The widespread poverty and misery of medieval people partially explains the resentment and suspicion toward those who had slightly more than others. And, inversely, those who had slightly more suspected their fellow villagers of casting envious, harmful looks in their direction. The church, charged with keeping order, commanded parishioners to focus on eternal bliss instead of coveting their neighbor's possessions or attempting to amass possessions of their own. Basil, one of the church fathers, warned Christians that the envious person risked losing paradise over a love of corruptible things (Basil 12). Or, as Saint Augustine put it, envy "burns up all virtues, dissipates all good, generates all evil" (14). Whenever harm came to anyone or anything, it was often retrospectively blamed on the envious gaze of a socially or economically marginalized person who, more often than not, turned out to be a woman.

As I will show in the following pages through a close analysis of textual examples from courtly and religious literature written between the late twelfth and the early fourteenth centuries, high medieval society was greatly concerned with harnessing the power of the female gaze. The commonality among the various texts examined here is that they all provide fragmentary cultural evidence of gazing ladies. Putting the pieces together, a clear picture emerges: within the larger system of patriarchy, a coherent societal subsystem was in place, regulating the female gaze by prohibiting and punishing covetous, envious, or sexual ogling. This gaze, as we saw in the discussion above, was believed to be highly disruptive to the societal system. One of the countermeasures taken is the direct interdiction of female gazing in texts such as Thomasin von Zerclaere's writing, *Der Renner*, Heinrich von

Melk's admonitions, and Der Stricker's morality tales (discussed in chapters 1 through 3). In the *Winsbeckin* text, the male-authored mother figure's subversive advice lays bare the patriarchal fear of uncontrolled female sexual gazing. Another countermeasure, working in unison with the explicit rules laid out in conduct literature, was the implicit stigmatizing of ogling ladies in courtly literature (as the examples in chapters 4 through 7 will show). While condemning the disruptive, disorderly sexual or probing female gaze, another form of looking was encouraged and rewarded because it supported medieval patriarchy: the motherly, admiring female gaze. Examples of this "good gaze" are found in the romances *Eneasroman, Parzival, Erec,* and *Iwein.* This subsystem functioned as a feedback mechanism and an inherent structural support of medieval *ordo.*

While literary texts, as well as historical and anthropological sources, confirm the existence of a universal dread of the probing female gaze, they do not explain it. The key to understanding why the patriarchal system placed such great importance on controlling the gaze of women by any means available is found only in psychoanalytic theory. Admittedly, the psychoanalytic approach is not without pitfalls and shortcomings. Freud was, no doubt, a product of his specific time and social class, writing from a male norm; recent scholarly reassessments of his contribution have downplayed its lasting influence and significance. Yet I believe that his sexism and errors are not central to psychoanalytic theory. Freudian texts and theories rightly are critiqued and revised, but because the core of the psychoanalytic approach is so useful, there is still no better way of laying bare the inner workings of patriarchal society. For feminism, Freud's discovery that there is nothing inevitable about sexual development was a breakthrough. It opened the door to an inquiry into societal roles that had simply been understood as biological and accepted as immutable, as a given. Hence, Freud's work is vital for feminist theory because it centralizes gender and sexuality. Psychoanalytic theory deals with femininity and masculinity; it is a theory of gender inequality. Women are made, not born, and biology does not suffice to explain sexual orientation and gender personality. Despite all its blemishes, psychoanalysis is still the best theory we have to demonstrate the function of the sociocultural organization of gender.

In *Visual and Other Pleasures,* Laura Mulvey, a feminist film studies scholar, uses specific psychoanalytic modes of inquiry regarding the gaze that proved particularly productive for my own exploration of the female gaze as represented in medieval texts. She bases her investigation on Freud's concepts of castration anxiety, scopophilia, and the fetish. She locates the origin of the love affair with gazing in the infant's look at the mother's face. This early gaze is not yet gendered. Or, more precisely, it is only gendered from one direction—the mother's. At this stage, both the male and the female infant display a strong and equal identification with the mother. Mulvey postulates a primordial pleasure of looking that has two contradictory aspects: one is voyeuristic, that is, pleasure comes from gazing at the human form; the other is narcissistic, that is, pleasure ensues from the identification with the visual object, much like looking in a mirror. These types represent the Freudian dichotomy of sexual instincts and ego libido. Mulvey does not examine why or how the initially ungendered infantile enjoyment of the mother's face turns into a male-gendered gazing position. Her goal is simply to describe and understand the state of affairs in a male-dominant society.

In "Women's Cinema as Counter-Cinema," one of Mulvey's contemporaries, Claire Johnston, also used a theoretical, psychoanalytic approach to understanding women's roles. According to Johnston, female characters in film do not represent "woman" but instead, by a process of displacement, the male phallus. "Woman" as woman is largely absent. As a sign, she becomes the pseudo-center of cinematic discourse, the trace of the exclusion and repression of Woman ("Women's Cinema" 33). This argument strongly links feminist film studies to feminist medieval studies. Some feminist medieval scholars came to the conclusion that "woman" did not exist in medieval texts either, and female figures stood for male-male relationships or male fantasy.[7] Johnston theorizes the female character as split into a symbol for both maternal plenitude and the threat of castration. The female gaze in medieval texts demonstrates a similar split into a good, maternal female gaze and a "bad," sexually active, and aggressive gaze.

Mulvey and the other feminist film theorists produced an important shift in analytic focus, away from a purely textual analysis and toward a concern with the structures of identification and visual pleasure. For my own investigation of the representation of gazing females in medieval texts, this is the most significant move—to get away from an analysis of the narrative and lay bare the psychological structures behind the cultural practice of viewing, showing how the gaze is constructed and to what degree the depiction of both male and female figures by a male writer/ director reflects a general pattern of how men wanted to see or be seen by women.

One attempt at this reformulation of the gender paradigm through the female gaze is found in feminist psychoanalytic writing. An important theorist in the Freudian line is Luce Irigaray. According to Irigaray, writing in *Speculum of the Other Woman*, the gaze is where it all begins. Without the male gaze there would be no horror of the female genitals, no fear of castration; without the female gaze there would be no knowledge of a lack, therefore no penis envy. The male gazer looks but sees nothing; there is only nothing, no thing, to be seen. The female gazer sees something, sees her own disadvantage. "Woman as mirror" represents what Irigaray calls the specular logic of patriarchy. Woman, caught in this paradigm, has two choices: either to remain silent or incoherent, or to enact the specular representation of herself. Women's choices, according to Irigaray, are limited to either incoherence or mimicry. If they submit to patriarchal logic according to which the male body is the norm, it is unavoidable that female sexual organs and also the female gaze are coded as "uncanny": creepy and disturbing. The female gaze, within this system of thought, is closely linked to envy. The lexeme "envy" is, through its Latin root "invidere," related to vision, as I have already pointed out above. "Woman" gazes at something she does not have and, therefore, becomes a threat to men who are in possession of the desired item. This perceived threat provides a psychoanalytic clue to the patriarchal prohibition against female gazing.

There is a strong similarity between Mulvey's reading of the male gaze and Irigaray's evaluation of patriarchal specularization. For both theorists, women are relegated to passivity within the male scopic economy. Women's visual enjoyment is either impossible or has to be pursued through a symbolic destruction of visual pleasure. If, as Freud stipulates, girls experience envy upon seeing male genitals, it follows logically that female gazing denotes a threat. Both looking at the female site of castration and being looked at by a "castrated being" would be highly undesirable and create the need for fetishization as well as other safeguards against envious female gazing.

Psychoanalytic theories provide valid insights into the meaning of the female gaze. However, only Donald Winnicott, in *Playing and Reality*, opens up a specific space within the exploration of human development that Freud neglected and from which another theory of the gaze emerges. Focusing on what Freud called the pre-oedipal phase, Winnicott's approach provides us with a way of theorizing the female gaze not as threatening and castrating but as nurturing, positive, and vitally important to normal development. It is this theory of the "good" maternal gaze that constitutes the other end of the spectrum in the conceptualization of the female gaze, explaining, I would argue, the paradoxical coexistent practices in medieval patriarchy of worshipping the Lady while simultaneously reviling female nature as such.

Winnicott's work focused on the importance of transitional objects and phenomena—the "first possessions"—in infant development. The transitional object is "some thing . . . that becomes vitally important to the infant . . . as a defense against anxiety" (4). He describes the special relationship between the infant and the object: The infant assumes control over an object chosen or provided by the adult caregivers. The object is both loved and mutilated, and should not be changed, unless changed by the infant. It must survive aggression, give warmth, move, or have texture to give the infant the impression that the object has a vitality of its own. The fate of the object is that it will gradually lose its meaning. The early attitude toward the transitional object is identical in boys and girls.

The purpose of the transitional object is that it equates with the breast. In objects-relations theory, the breast, not the penis, is the primary physical identifier of sexuality. The object signifies the tangible presence of what Winnicott calls the "good-enough mother," less in a symbolical than in an actual and material way. It is noteworthy that the true transitional object is more important than the mother herself, since it is, from the infant's viewpoint, part of the infant and, therefore, inseparable from him or her. Winnicott emphasizes how every infant needs the mother's presence and her loving gaze for the formation of a healthy psyche. The infant must feel as if he or she is the center of the universe, perfect in the eyes of the mother. The mother's face is the infant's first mirror; when the baby looks at the mother's face he or she sees him- or herself. Actually, the infant is reflected twice in the mother's eyes: first literally, her eyes functioning as a mirror, a reflective surface, and then again figuratively, in the way she looks at him or her. The psychological mirroring of the mother has been clinically observed in the way mothers, in a spontaneous gesture, mimic an infant's facial expressions. This mimesis creates an awareness of self-representation and prepares the infant for later social relations.[8] If the infant does not enjoy a loving, uncritical motherly gaze, neurosis results. Clinical evidence points to the fact that a child whose primary narcissism is disturbed by inadequacies of parental care responds by a need for constant reassurance, a need to be watched and admired; the child develops a narcissism that will not be outgrown. It is this supportive motherly gaze that is constantly and narcissistically requested by male personages in medieval male-authored texts.

This argument becomes somewhat problematic, however, because, according to Winnicott's theory, the early gaze of the "good-enough mother" is necessary for both male and female development. Hence, if a postulated medieval lack of meticulous and loving infant care produced narcissistic human beings that craved the approving motherly gaze, should this not have caused the same effect in female children?

Nancy Chodorow's theory might provide an answer to the conundrum. In *Feminism and Psychoanalytic Theory*, Chodorow deplores, first of all, that the mother's role in subject formation within patriarchal society has been inadequately researched. Psychoanalytic scholarship often overlooked the fact that the mother is not merely a nongendered, neutral unit to fill children's needs; she is also a person, specifically, a subject of the female sex. It is true that Freud tentatively claimed a gendering of the mother's attitude toward her child. However, he suggests that her relationship to a son is superior to the one she might have with a daughter, since it involves less ambivalence (Chodorow, *Feminism* 26). I would disagree with this conclusion. It is likely that mothers identify more readily with their daughters and, based on the similarity they share, develop a closer and longer-lasting mutual connection. From the point of view of the female child, there is simply no need for an immediate and radical breach with the mother in the process of individualization, while a boy must sever himself irreversibly from his mother and her world in order to become a man. This separation causes an injury to the male psyche, and since the male is in charge of patriarchal society and culture, he constructs them around the attempt to heal the wound. Manly pursuits become coded as better, more relevant than anything the mother, sister, or nurse does, and these ladies better pay attention when he performs his spectacular feats. After all, they owe it to him for excluding him from their sphere. He now needs their adoring gaze to be reassured in his otherness, his maleness. If there is no female gaze approving or confirming a man's achievement, it is as if it didn't happen.

By defining male as "not-female" in the absence of real male role models, the boy inevitably needs to distance himself from the realm he inhabited since birth. He has to violently reject, even revile, characteristics considered feminine to differentiate himself, to become the male personage he created in opposition to his female caregivers. Unconsciously, however, he will retain an idealized image of the mother, of "paradise lost." He excludes himself, but once he becomes initiated into the male sphere he will, in turn, exclude women from it. Abjection and marginality describe this specific process of individuation. Abjection is the operation of the psyche through which identity is constituted by excluding anything that threatens its borders. In patriarchal society, the main threat to the development of male identity is dependence upon the maternal body, which must be abjected. It follows that the primary identification of both male and female children is with the mother or female caregiver. Her mothering, in turn, is gendered as well, reproducing herself in a girl, while preparing a boy, indirectly, for his male role, apart from her and her realm.

I believe that it is this conflict, this violent and painful early separation of the male child from his mother, that acts as a feedback loop in the vicious cycle of the creation and re-creation of the systemic submission and abjection of women.

In the following chapters I will provide textual evidence of how the female gaze was regulated in medieval culture and society, and how writings from sermons, conduct literature, and courtly romance worked in unison toward the preservation of patriarchal structures. The goal of maintaining the societal system—medieval *ordo*—is where the purpose of the clerical and courtly texts intersect. Sexually coded direct eye contact initiated by a girl was feared to result in illicit and undesirable physical attraction between two people of unequal social standing. Obviously, a girl choosing a spouse based on visual attraction would have upended the patriarchal system in which girls served as objects of exchange toward the creation of bonds between men.

1

"A lady should never look directly at a male visitor"

THOMASIN VON ZERCLAERE

To the medieval mind, the potential of the female gaze to subvert existing power structures was all too real, and attempts were made to contain and control it. Girls were taught from earliest childhood to avert their eyes and to avoid ogling or staring.[1] Evidence of these preemptive measures survives in the form of educational manuals. The popularity of such texts is proven by the relatively large amount of extant manuscripts. Among some of the more notable didactic authors outside the German language area are Robert de Blois, Philippe de Novare, and Vincent de Beauvais. The latter particularly emphasized the importance of strict moral training of noble girls.

In the following chapters I discuss five of the most widely circulated didactic works: *Der Welsche Gast* by Thomasin von Zerclaere, *Winsbeckin* by an anonymous author, *Der Renner* by Hugo von Trimberg, *Von des todes gehugde* by Heinrich von Melk, and a didactic poem by Der Stricker, "Die Eingemauerte Frau." Even though these texts were not exclusively written to teach female conduct, they do include long didactic passages on how women should or should not gaze. All the authors of these texts are male, but they represent a broad range of clerical and courtly viewpoints on female conduct. How their authoritative message—composed by men who had little contact with girls—was received by the majority of female readers is not known. The life of a woman in thirteenth-century Europe probably differed dramatically from what we can glean from the textual norms the conduct writers attempted to establish. Nonetheless, these writings provide valuable insight into customs, mentalities, and expectations. For the twelfth and thirteenth centuries in western Europe, only the conduct writers' side of the story is preserved; for later periods, scholars are fortunate to have evidence of actual social practices recorded in personal letters or court papers.

"Weil die weibliche Natur so schwach war, mussten Frauen sorgfältiger belehrt und angeleitet werden als Männer" (Bumke, *Höfische Kultur* 470; Because female nature was so weak, women had to be taught and guided more thoroughly than men). With this statement, the German medievalist Joachim Bumke sums up the general stance of the church fathers, influenced by the well-established belief in a hierarchical order between the sexes as explained by Isidor of Seville in his *Etymologiae*. Isidor based his findings on observations of the animal kingdom, concluding that the main physical difference between the sexes is male strength and female weakness. Medieval thinkers and writers built on the perception of the superior male body as proof of their right and obligation to dominate women, the weaker sex, in all areas of life.

Noble girls were kept busy with women's work: spinning, weaving, and stitching. Keeping a girl in a state of childlike innocence was not an easy task; even the sight of her own nudity could trigger undesirable physical urges. There are passages in the conduct manual by Vincent de Beauvais, *De Eruditione Filiorum Nobilium*, written for Louis IX of France, where he pleads with parents to lock away their unmarried daughters to safeguard their virginity. According to Vincent, parents should use classical and scriptural examples in teaching their daughters to remain chaste. He thought it best to curtail female public appearances; the weaker sex needed to be protected from temptations. Vincent disapproved of all forms of female amusement and even insisted that wives should refrain from seeking gratification in marital intercourse. As a prevention of sensual enjoyment, he advised parents not to allow their daughters to bathe frequently. All other pleasures of the flesh, such as eating, drinking, laughing, talking, and extended periods of rest, put a girl's purity at risk. The gaze of a girl, according to Vincent, is an indicator of her chastity, or lack thereof. If she strays, her eyes will give her away, so she is well advised to keep her gaze fixed on the ground. Her eyes are not supposed to see, nor are they supposed to be seen.

A detailed account of what society might have expected of well-bred young men and women in the thirteenth century is recorded in the didactic poem of Thomasin von Zerclaere, *Der Welsche Gast*. This work is subdivided into ten parts, containing about ten chapters each. The first part concerns itself with the teaching of rules for proper conduct, including *Minnelehre* (teachings about love). The next part focuses on the teaching of morality, which, according to Thomasin, is always based on *staete* (constancy), the most important virtue. A virtuous person supports and defends the God-given order and resists change. *Mâze, reht und milte* (moderation, justice and mercy) closely follow *staete* in importance.

In his prologue, Thomasin introduces himself to his readership and lays out his beliefs and goals. He strongly holds that reading *guotiu maere* (morality tales) has a formative effect on a person's character. One of his objectives is to communicate such wisdom to his audience, starting with the moral imperative that every man should follow the good advice found in books:

Ein ieglîch man sich vlîzen sol
Daz ers ervüll mit guoter tât
Swaz er guots gelesen hât. (ll. 3–5)

(Every man/everyone should try his best to put the good things he reads into practice.)

Thomasin is using "man" in the generic; he later specifies that he expects "beidiu wîp unde man" (both women and men) to improve their character by listening to appropriate instruction. He insists on the Aristotelian idea of purification through identification with personages from literature, and he seems particularly attracted to the Arthurian cycle:

Ich heiz Thomasîn von Zerclaere
boeser liute spot ist mir unmaere
Hân ich Gâweins hulde wol,
von reht mîn Key spotten sol (ll. 75–78)

(My name is Thomasin of Zerclaere, and the disrespect of certain people means nothing to me. If I have the respect of Gawain, Key can mock me all he wants.)

Gâwein is presented as the ideal Arthurian knight whom every man should emulate, while the ill-mannered Sir Key stands for discourteous conduct and lack of chivalry. Even though the Arthurian characters were likely composed in part for the very purpose of serving as role models, Thomasin was the first writer of conduct literature to use them explicitly as such. However, he did so with a caveat, declaring them to be of limited and preliminary didactic usefulness; once young people had come *ze sinne*, to intellectual maturity, an engagement with the world of *aventiure* was, according to Thomasin, no longer productive.

One of the most significant and much repeated admonitions in *Der Welsche Gast* is to respect visiting strangers (the title of the work translates as "The visiting stranger"). This command is meant for both men and women:

Bêde vrouwen unde herren
sulen vrömede liute êren.
Ist sîn ein vrömeder man niht wert,
si habent sich selben geêrt.
Ist sîn aver wert der,
sô habent si sîn bêde êr. (ll. 377–82)

(Both ladies and lords should honor strangers. Even if a stranger doesn't deserve it, the honor they extend will reflect back on them. If he is worthy, though, they will all benefit from the honor.)

Thomasin underlines the social and moral importance of extending hospitality. Failing to do so was unthinkable. Until restaurants and hotels became prevalent in the latter part of the thirteenth century, traveling strangers depended on the *milte* (generosity) of estate owners to feed and house them upon request. Even though this custom affected everyone, ladies needed special guidance and strictly defined limits for their comportment with visiting male travelers. Thomasin begins his gender-specific admonitions with instructions regarding her role as both the object and subject of the gaze:

Ein vrouwe sol sich sehen lân,
kumt zir ein vrömeder man.
Swelihiu sich niht sehen lât,
diu sol ûz ir kemenât

sîn allenthalben unerkant;
büeze alsô, sî ungenant.
Ein vrouwe sol niht vrevelîch
schimphen, daz stât vröuwelîch.
Ich wil ouch des verjehen,
ein vrouwe sol niht vast an sehen
einn vrömeden man, daz stât wol.
Ein edel juncherre sol
bêde rîter unde vrouwen
gezogenlîche gerne schouwen (ll. 391–404)

(A lady should let herself be seen if a stranger comes to her. The one who does not allow herself to be seen should remain unknown outside of her bedchamber and should suffer thus, unnamed. A lady should not use mockery; that is unbecoming. I must also proclaim that a lady should not gaze directly at a stranger, which is inappropriate. A young nobleman may politely look at both knights and ladies.)

Thomasin, curiously, insists that the lady offer herself as an object of the gaze while not permitting her to directly look at a male stranger herself. Was presenting a pleasing visual object to a weary male traveler part of the expected hospitality service? Thomasin seems to insinuate as much. While the lady was supposed to show herself without gazing, the young nobleman is encouraged to look at both "rîter unde vrouwen." Thomasin's encouragement of male ogling establishes unequivocally that approval or disapproval of the gaze depends on the gender of the looker; direct male gazing is permitted, while direct female gazing is not.

In his instructions on how to properly ride a horse, Thomasin takes up the subject of the lady's gaze again:

Ein vrouwe sol recken niht ir hant,
swenn si rît, vür ir gewant;
si sol ir ougen und ir houbet
stille haben, daz geloubet. (ll. 437–40)

(A lady should not stick her hand out of her coat while riding. Her eyes and her head should remain still, believe that.)

She should not gaze, but neither should she expose herself too much to the gaze of men:

Wil sich ein vrouwe mit zuht bewarn,
si sol niht âne hülle varn.
Si sol ir hül ze samen hân,
ist si der garnatsch ân.
Lât si am lîbe iht sehen par,
daz ist wider zuht gar. (ll. 451–56)

(If a lady wants to keep with good manners, she should not go out without a cape. She should hold it together in front if she is not wearing a long robe beneath it. If she shows any part of her body at all, that is against good form.)

The lady is to remain an unspecified, cloaked object of the gaze, without showing any specific body parts. Thomasin requires noble female readers of his conduct manual to resemble the generic apparitions we also find in courtly poetry and romance.

Devoid of specific markers of female beauty, immovable and fully covered by her robe and her cape, she is neutralized as a temptation and a threat to medieval order. He continues:

Ein vrouwe sol niht hinder sich
dicke sehen, dunket mich.
Si sol gên vür sich geriht
und sol vil umbe sehen niht; (ll. 459–62)

(I think that a lady should not often look behind herself. She should go straight ahead and shouldn't look around much.)

Thomasin considers it bad form for a woman to let her eyes wander while traveling on horseback. She is to ride without movement, holding still, while looking straight ahead. The way she rides is to show to the world that she is brought up with *zuhte*, the strength of good morals and self-control; she will not be tempted by the sights and sounds around her, nor will she tempt visiting strangers. The passage calls to mind a biblical example (Genesis 19) of a woman disobeying the explicit divine prohibition against looking; I am referring, of course, to Lot's wife, who could not resist turning around to look at her burning home one last time and paid with her life for this act of defiance.

In the next verses, Thomasin emphasizes that a properly raised young woman should speak rarely, and only when spoken to:

Ein juncvrouwe sol selten iht
sprechen, ob mans vrâget niht.
Ein vrouwe sol ouch niht sprechen vil,
ob si mir gelouben wil,
und benamen swenn si izzet,
sô sol si sprâchen niht, daz wizzet. (ll. 465–70)

(A young lady should rarely speak, and only when she is asked a question. A lady should not talk much, either, if she gives any credence to my teaching, and especially while she is eating she should not speak at all, know this.)

To summarize Thomasin's instructions for girls and women: a lady should allow herself to be seen, modestly covered up by long robes and capes, but she should never make eye contact with a man who is not her husband; she should speak only rarely, if at all. One explanation of these manners-based prohibitions, again, is found in the variety of possible sexual consequences of unrestrained female gazing. Medieval conduct writers discouraged any form of female pleasure seeking, fearing it would eventually lead to graver missteps. If a woman let her eyes wander freely, casting looks at men, her visual enjoyment might not only trigger her own sexual desire but also attract and embolden the visiting male stranger, sending him signals he might read as consent to adultery. Naturally, under patriarchal rule and the inheritance system of primogeniture, female promiscuity was a catastrophic threat because of the potentially resulting illegitimate pregnancy. The social defense mechanism put into place to prevent this ruinous chain of events, caused by ravenous, uncontrolled and uncanny female sexual urges, was *huote*.[2]

The various translation choices of *huote* in modern German include "Schutz, Obhut, Fürsorge, Überwachung, Bewachung, Aufsicht" (protection, custody, care, surveillance, guard, supervision). The first three choices are euphemisms; the latter three more accurately describe this frequently related medieval practice of policing women. *Huote* of ladies is a trope of medieval literature. Sometimes, *huote* appeared in personified form; it was transformed from an abstract concept into a human agent of surveillance. The main purpose of *huote* was always to ensure that women did not step outside the social boundaries. Supervision of wives not only protected holy matrimony but stabilized the medieval system of *ordo* as a whole. Der Stricker, in his tale "Die Unbewachte Gattin" (*Erzählungen* 190–203), mocks the times of courtly love when husbands had lost the good sense of practicing *huote*. He claims that wise men have always kept a keen eye on their wives and strictly controlled their lustful gaze. He regrets that some men, out of fear of public criticism, have begun allowing their housewives to freely ogle male guests:

> Hie vor, dô man diu huote schalt
> und des sumelich wirt sêre engalt,
> daz er lie sîne hûsvrouwen
> di geste gerne schouwen,
> dô si ir triuwe übersach
> und ir reht und ir ê zebrach—
> daz hiez hôchgemuotiu minne. (ll. 1–7)

> (Once, when huote was held in low regard, each host suffered bitterly for allowing his wife to ogle male guests, which made her forget her faithfulness and break the marriage vows—they called that "high-minded love.")

The dreaded result of this reckless lack of control over one's wife is an offense to God and the ruin of the marriage.

The romances also contain evidence of female characters who, if left unsupervised, invariably indulge in adulterous affairs. Two of the better-known examples are Tristan's lover, Isolde, and Arthur's queen, Guinevere. The most powerful rhetorical argument against *huote*, however, is found in Gottfried von Strassburg's *Tristan*. Here, the narrator makes the case that *huote* is counterproductive: the more one supervises the illicit lovers, the more pleasure they derive from their forbidden games:

> und swer in daz spil leiden wil,
> weiz got der liebet in daz spil.

sô man s'ie harter dannen nimet,
sô sî des spiles ie mê gezimet
und sô s'ie harter clebent an (ll. 17827–32)

(And whoever wants to spoil their pleasure, God knows, actually heightens it for them. The harder one tries to keep them from it, the more they enjoy their little game, the more they get attached to it.)

An adulteress is not held back by inner restraint, or she would not commit adultery in the first place; she will invariably break through the barriers of external control. A good and faithful wife, on the other hand, does not need to be watched by others, since she watches herself:

der guoten darf man hüeten niht,
si hüetet selbe, als man giht.
und swer ir hüetet über daz,
entriuwen der ist ir gehaz. (ll. 17875–78)

(The good wife needs no surveillance; she keeps an eye on herself, as they say. She will surely hate whoever supervises her beyond that.)

This argument is somewhat ironically echoed in Gawain's speech to Iwein. Of course, Gawain's intention is not to praise the goodness and faithfulness of Lady Laudine but rather to motivate his friend to leave her and join him in his adventures. Gawain strongly disagrees with the practice of *huote* and utters harsh words against excessive supervision of wives:

ein wîp die man hât erkant
in alsô staetem muote,
diu bedarf niht mêre huote
niuwan ir selber êren.
man sol die huote kêren
an irriu wîp und an kint,
diu sô einvaltec sint
daz sî eins alten wîbes rât
bringen mac ze missetât. (ll. 2890–98)

(A woman who has shown herself to be faithful no longer requires any chaperone other than her own honor. Supervision should be reserved for erring wives and young girls who are so simpleminded that they can be led astray by the advice of an old woman.)

Female self-supervision is, of course, a variation of the acceptable, desirable female gaze: self-scrutiny for the purpose of upholding patriarchal morality. Being Eve's daughter, however, a woman is forever tempted to engage in an activity simply because it is explicitly forbidden. The purpose of standing up against *huote* in the *excursus* above is not to defend women and their dignity but to warn the male reader of the futility of the practice. Women's obstinate and contrary nature will without fail drive them to escape watchdogs and break society's moral rules.

A psychoanalytic explanation for the strict regulation of women's gazing lies in what Nancy Chodorow describes as the "unstable male gender identity," continually in need of being reinforced and propped up by the undivided attention of mothers, girlfriends, or wives. The root of this narcissism is found in early childhood and personality development of males. Women's gender identity is more stable than that of men, who continually have to prove and defend maleness. Also, as an aside, it is worth remembering that the gaze as an indicator of social relationships is not unique to human beings. Among all mammals, staring is perceived as dominant and aggressive behavior, while looking down and avoiding the probing look of an opponent is understood as a sign of weakness and submission. Animals showing deference to others are usually younger, smaller, and weaker. This "animalistic" and simplistic explanation of a hierarchical order was already observed by Isidor of Seville. Medieval patriarchal leaders built on the perception of the superior male body as proof of their right and obligation to dominate women, the weaker sex, in all areas of life, in the name of a God-given order. Once the power structure was in place, it became a self-supporting system in which any form of disorder or dissent was considered a direct attack on God's will.

2

"Wilꝺ glances"

WINSBECKIN AND *DER RENNER*

The male author of the *Winsbeckin* text depicts a conversation between a girl and her mother about how to navigate through life without running afoul of medieval society's standards of decency.[1] Recently published collections—for instance, Mark Johnston's anthology *Medieval Conduct Literature*—have included the *Winsbeckin* text as a work of conduct literature. At first glance this designation seems justified, since the text treats the education of a young woman. A closer reading, though, reveals this classification as problematic. *Winsbeckin* is, I believe, not conduct literature at all but rather a misogynist attempt at parody of the conduct genre, specifically of the preceding *Der Winsbecke* text. The dubious advice given by the mother character is too subversive and too hyperbolic to be taken at face value. For our purposes, however, the text is quite illuminating: it illustrates the male author's fear and dread of female sexuality; it stands for patriarchal suspicion and mistrust of women's secret dealings in general, and the desire to suppress the female sexual gaze in particular.

The *Winsbeckin* text is attached to the didactic poem *Der Winsbecke*, attributed to an anonymous author referred to as "der tugendhafte schrîber," a nobleman from Windsbach in the Frankish region. The poem contains conduct advice from an old knight to his son. Chivalry and love, proper behavior toward one's fellow men, ladies, and clergy are central concerns. *Der Winsbecke* is a true piece of didactic writing advocating laudable qualities such as loyalty, compassion, truth, and generosity. It emphasizes a knight's dual obligation of serving both the world and God.

The *Winsbeckin* text, which is linguistically and poetically inferior to *Der Winsbecke*, portrays a dialogue between a mother and her daughter; the mother character attempts to indoctrinate the girl in what she considers advantageous conduct in society, especially concerning courtship and matrimony. The most important thing in life, according to this male-authored female personage, is to keep up *appearances* of honor and virtue in order to trick a man into marriage. As the mother shares her questionable wisdom with her daughter, her main message is that a young girl can achieve happiness and a good life only if she publicly if not genuinely conforms to the male ideal of a woman. Looking/gazing plays a significant role in this instrumentalization—in particular, the specific emphasis the mother places on something she calls "wilde blicke" (wild gazing).

The first mention of the female gaze occurs in the third verse: "wol mich, daz ich dich ie gesach!" (stanza 1, l. 3; I am blessed that I ever saw you!). The mother character, in a peculiar *laudatio* of her daughter's appearance, mimics a suitor's voice, announcing how blessed she was for having caught sight of the girl and not, as would seem more logical, by knowing her, being related to her, or having brought her into the world. She hyperbolically equates her daughter's familiar vision with the glorious arrival of spring. This comical simile, which is best understood as a parody of courtly love poetry, foreshadows how the mother character attempts to indoctrinate her daughter with a mocking patriarchal viewpoint: keeping up both her appearance and appearances will allow her to deceive and seduce male onlookers.

The daughter's response picks up her mother's preoccupation with looking and being looked at. After the elder Winsbeckin admonishes the younger to praise God, the girl replies:

Des volge ich, liebiu muoter, dir,
ich lobe in, so ich beste kan.
er sol der sinne helfen mir,
daz ich in sehe mit vorhten an (stanza 2, ll. 1–4)

(I will follow your advice on that, dear Mother, I shall praise Him as best I can. He shall help my senses so that I can gaze upon Him with fear.)

Her worship of God is naively vision-based: "that I can gaze upon him with fear." The cynical narrator portrays the girl as an innocent simpleton. She appears sweet enough; she is obedient and submissive to her mother, respectful of the authorities, and eager to learn. Her mother's instruction in women's guile has not yet corrupted the girl, but, the narrator seems to imply, just give it some time; she is female, after all.

In the fifth stanza, after a brief and perfunctory nod to the virtues of modesty and moderation, the mother gives her daughter an emphatic warning against the sending of "wild gazes":

schiuz wilder blicke niht ze vil,
da lose merker bî dir sîn (stanza 5, ll. 1 and 2)

(Don't shoot off too many wild gazes,
because spies are always around you.)

The verb connected to the gaze is quite significant here: "schiezen" (to shoot), which can be translated into modern German as "schießen/ schleudern/ werfen . . . an-, niederschießen, treffen; töten; erlegen; abschießen" (Hennig). All those lexemes have the connotation of aggression and violence, even murder. As I mentioned in the introduction, the act of looking had a very concrete, material, and probing quality in the premodern understanding; "Blicke" are like bullets; they are shot, they are cast, they pierce and they kill. The noun "blic," in addition to retaining the modern connotation of "Blick" (glance, look, gaze) is, in Middle High German, associated with danger and aggression: "swertes blic," for example, meaning "Schwertstreich" (attack with the sword), and "viures blic," meaning "Funke" (spark). The central point of the mother's admonition is not forbidding her daughter to indulge in this form of visual aggression; she merely wants her to rein it in. More than anything, the mother worries about a stain on her daughter's reputation. "Lose merker"—cunning spies, as Ann Marie Rasmussen translates it—surround them, ever ready to censure the girl's conduct, ever ready to cast doubt on her virginity. Ironically, girls are constantly observed and ogled by the self-appointed watchdogs who consider female gazing inappropriate. But what about their own probing stares? To avoid those suspicious and damaging spying eyes, the mother character warns against frequent "wild" gazing. The real danger, the mother cautions, lies not in ogling men or, for that matter, in immorality, but in "being seen while ogling men." Improper conduct is only wrong when the unseemly act enters the public domain. The established societal order remains intact if infractions are isolated cases and if pains are taken to keep up the appearance of virtue. In other words, this misogynist male-authored dialogue between female characters aims to expose women's profound mendacity and immorality; the female sex, the text clearly states, generally accepts and even encourages impure and immoral gazing as long as it happens surreptitiously. This morally bankrupt lesson is taught by the mother character, training her daughter not in righteousness but in duplicity, coaching her not on how to openly rebel against the system but on how to subvert it underhandedly. The male author takes great pains to underline, through hyperbole and biting humor, the hypocrisy and dishonesty of women attempting to appear more virtuous than they are.

The simpleminded daughter character at first fails to grasp her mother's amoral advice. In the sixth stanza she asks her mother to clearly define what she means by "wilde blicke":

> bewîse, liebiu muoter, mich
> der rede baz (ich bin niht wîs),
> wie wilde blicke sîn gestalt,
> wie, wâ ich die vermîden sül,
> daz si mich machen iht ze balt. (stanza 6, ll. 6–10)

(Dear Mother, explain your speech to me better, I am not wise; what is the nature of these wild gazes, how and where should I avoid them so that they don't make me too bold.)

The daughter asks how she can possibly avoid wild gazing if she does not know what it is. Finally, in the seventh stanza, the mother supplies her daughter with her definition of "wilde blicke" and also, for good measure, throws in a behavioral code regarding female gazing; it is a lesson that she herself supposedly learned as a young woman at court:

> Ez heizent wilde blicke wol,
> als ich ze hove bewîset bin,
> als ein wîp vür sich sehen sol,

daz ir diu ougen vliegent hin,
sam ob si habe unstaeten sin,
und âne mâze daz geschiht.
daz ist ir lobe ein ungewin:
die melder merkent unser site.
twinc dîniu ougen deste baz,
daz râte ich, tohter, unde bite. (stanza 7, ll. 1–10)

(Wild gazing, as I learned myself at court, is when a woman looks around so wildly that her eyes are flying here and there as if she were quite flighty, and when it happens without measure it speaks very much against her. We are always being watched, so control your eyes as best you can, I advise and pray of you, daughter.)

Wild gazing occurs, the mother explains, when a girl's eyes wander all over the place, instead of being modestly fixed on the ground. Wild gazing signals "unstaeten sin," a flighty, unreliable, and promiscuous character. The focus of the lesson, again, is not virtue itself but the practice of appearing virtuous in public. The mother begs her daughter to control herself and not reveal her hidden sexual urges. She is not just concerned for the girl; her own reputation would suffer right along with her daughter's if the latter were caught in the act of ogling men.

In her speech, the male-authored mother character equates woman and her body—a standard misogynist trope. A woman's moral, ethical, and intellectual persona are determined by her physical nature. Her demeanor speaks volumes about her character, and her body is an open book; its text was written before she was born. Textual assumptions of "women are like . . ." predate the musings of the *Winsbeckin* writer. Alcuin Blamires assembled a useful anthology of misogynist medieval texts from the twelfth to the fifteenth centuries, titled *Women Defamed and Women Defended*. He includes specific classical texts that affected clerical attitudes toward women in the Middle Ages and provided the roots and the substructure of the antifeminist tradition. Greek physiology as taught by Aristotle, for example, stated that the male principle is soul and form, while the female principle is body and matter; this line of thought doubtlessly supplied the scholarly rationale for medieval gender divisions and the belief in the inferiority of women.

It is more complicated than this, though. For example, it is not clear whether the moral watchdogs, the "maerkere and melder," were mainly female or male. There is a high likelihood that they were women.[2] The control of women's sexuality—in particular, the suppression of female sexual gazing—was enforced by female agents of patriarchy. Chodorow writes that "women's motherhood and mothering role seem to be the most important features in accounting for the universal secondary status of women" (*Feminism* 34). The *Winsbeckin* text confirms this near-universal truth.

In the thirteenth stanza, the mother character reveals to the daughter that her success in society depends primarily on whether men will desire her. The meek obedience and purity she displays publicly will serve this all-important purpose:

> wis staeter site, von herzen guot,
> sô hâstû guoter liute segen.
> mahtû die tugent ûf gewegen,
> dir wirt von manegem werden man
> mit wûnschen nâhen bî gelegen. (stanza 13, ll. 3–7)

> (Be steady and good, that way you will have the blessing of good people. If you can muster up this type of virtue, many a nobleman will desire to sleep with you.)

Rasmussen interprets these verses as reinforcing the message of how asexual female behavior increases male desire (*Mothers and Daughters* 142). While this may be true, I am more suspicious of this text and believe that we should not take it at its word. I read the hyperbolic speech of the mother as an attempt to highlight women's perverse view of virtue as a means to an end: the bed of a nobleman. In addition to being a misogynist statement, it is also an indictment of medieval society, a harsh "Ständekritik"; the narrator sarcastically raises the issue of the blatant hypocrisy of courtly behavior.

In the fifteenth stanza of the *Winsbeckin* poem, the mother enlightens her daughter that it is the male gaze that determines a woman's value. If he likes what he sees, she is worthy, she has exchange value (stanza 15, ll. 4–10). Here, a mother teaches her daughter that appearing chaste is more important than being chaste; the older woman initiates her daughter into the feminine world of trickery, treachery, and lies. The girl may ogle and lust after beautiful male bodies as long as others, especially the self-appointed moral watchdogs, are not aware of it. The mother character represents, in a satiric way, the embodiment of what men (like the male author) dread most about women. As boys they were pushed out of the space belonging to their mother, their nurse, and their sisters; they had to learn maleness by contrasting themselves to women. They eventually excluded women from their own pursuits, creating and supporting a system in which women were inferior, all the while resenting their expulsion from the female realm, longing for female approval and the loving, nonjudgmental motherly gaze. The author of this parody of medieval conduct literature laid bare the deepest fear of patriarchal agents: that women had, through their treacherous secrecy passed from one generation to the next, developed a subversive way to get the better of men, after all.

Another medieval literary text concerned with the regulation of the female gaze is Hugo von Trimberg's *Der Renner*. The text is one of the longest didactic works of the Middle Ages, and it is preserved in seventy-two extant manuscripts—proof of its overwhelming popularity.[3]

Hugo von Trimberg spent more than four decades of his life as a schoolmaster at Sankt Gangolf in Bamberg. Unlike Thomasin von Zerclaere, Hugo did not write for a noble, secular audience. His texts are strongly marked by religion and morality, and he harshly judges both worldly nobles and the staff in their service. He does not spare clerics, maintaining that they are the sinners most in need of repentance. In Hugo's view, no one is righteous and everyone has to repent of something.

Of interest to this inquiry is that *Der Renner* takes great pains to excoriate girls for looking at men; the concern with female gazing is so considerable that extracts of the text were circulated independently under a title that foregrounded the thematic: *Dy spehen mayd*. Much like the examples of literature focusing on the education of young nobles, *Der Renner* admonishes contemporary readers to uphold the order and the system structuring their social world. This didactic text's most fundamental message is that, despite the many wrongs committed by powerful and influential individuals, *ordo* is God-ordained and eternal; it must be respected and maintained.

After some introductory allegorical embellishments, the narrator begins his argument at the beginning: Adam and Eve. Surprisingly, he initially refrains from using the common trope of solely blaming the first woman for the eviction from Paradise. As a cleric, he was surely aware that many of the church fathers, such as Saint Ambrose, ascribed guilt for the original sin to Eve alone (Blamires 61). Instead, the narrator teaches that Adam was liable as well:

Wêrn si beliben wîse
Und hêten behalten sîn gebot:
Sô wêrn wir frî vor aller nôt. (ll. 120–22)

(If they had stayed wise and kept His commandment, we would be free of all suffering.)

The narrator deplores that the first couple overstepped the God-given boundaries; it was a rather costly mistake for them and their descendants. A few verses later he does allude that it was mainly Eve who brought sin into the world, but only to remind us that Mary, another woman, canceled it out by giving birth to Christ. The juxtaposition of the two figures, Eve and Mary, lies, of course, at the very heart of the paradoxical medieval stance on women. The condemnation of Eve as the one who lost paradise for mankind, and the worship of Mary, the perfect virgin and mother of Christ who earned it back, determined the educated and educational discourse, clerical and courtly, of the day.

Even though the text initially spreads the blame, it quickly turns to lamenting female vices and specifically deplores "wilde und unstaete meiden":

Kurzen muot und langez hâr
Habent die meide sunderbar,
Diu wal machet in daz herze blint.
Diu ougen zeigent in den wec,
Von den ougen gêt ein stec
Zuo dem herzen, niht gar lanc.
Uf den stîget manic gedanc,
Wen si nemen oder niht.
Ouwê wie dicke daz geschiht (ll. 309–17)

(Strangely, girls seem to have short morals and long hair; choices make their hearts blind and they allow themselves to be guided by their eyes. From their eyes it is only a short path to their heart; on that path many thoughts wander; they think about whom they should or should not take. Woe, how often it happens like that.)

The narrator chides girls for awarding their affection based on a man's appearance, not his character; their eyes misguide them in their choices, while their hearts are blind. Clearly, the female gaze and reason are incompatible. He proceeds to give a lengthy list of the types of good men who might be unfairly rejected for lack of physical appeal or for other superficial criteria (below I am quoting only twelve of the list's seventy-six lines):

Diz ist zem êrsten ir gedanc:
Dirre ist kurz, jener ist lanc;
Einer ist bartoht und ist alt,
Der ander junc und übel gestalt;
Dirre ist mager unde smal,
Der ist veizet, jener ist kal;
Dirre ist edel, der ist swach,
Jener selten sper zebrach;
Einer ist wîz, der ander ist swarz,
Sô heizet einer meister Harz;
Der ist bleich, dirre ist rôt,
Jener izzet selten froelich brôt (ll. 321–32)

(Those are her first thoughts: this one is short, that one is tall; one is bearded and old, another is young but ugly; this one is skinny and narrow, that one is fat, that one is bald, this one is noble, but that one is weak; that one has not broken many spears; one is white, one is black; this one is named Master Harz; this one is pale, this one is ruddy, the one over there is rarely in a good mood.)

Not surprisingly, the text fails to list worthy women rejected by men for similarly superficial reasons. The narrator's catalogue contains the clear expectation that the female gaze should, ideally, be noncritical and loving. A woman's look should not stop at the surface, but she should see and love a man for who he really is. This male-authored expectation is echoed throughout conduct literature and courtly romance. A good woman gazes lovingly, not critically, like a good mother, or the young girl in Hartmann's tale *Der arme Heinrich*.

Sarah Westphal engages with this text's harsh judgment of the critical female gaze in her book *Textual Poetics of German Manuscripts, 1300–1500*. She comments on the inversion contained in the poem's title, which was most likely added by someone involved in the production: "The idea of young women seeing and judging their counterparts in the male world is nearly inadmissible from the standpoint of most estates literature, in which even the passive stance of women's being seen by men, and still more their desire to be seen, is condemned as the source of moral turpitude in unmarried women and the first step toward hell" (155).

Critically gazing females constitute a threat to medieval social order, since they refuse to blindly accept men and circumstances as they find them. They represent a disruptive agency. As our narrator laments, gazing girls have poor judgment and should be strictly discouraged from expressing or even having an opinion. This power to judge, after all, is the divine prerogative of male members of society.

Reading those passages against the grain, though, the text implies that the girls whom the narrator admonishes actually appear to have a choice in the selection of a partner. In the lines above we detect no direct criticism of the girls for ogling men, as in Thomasin von Zerclaere's writing, but only the mention of inappropriate criteria girls apply in selecting the object of their affection. If they must gaze, they should do so uncritically—that sums up the lesson of this text.

The narrator proceeds to deplore both the vanity and the laziness of those superficial girls who would rather show off their braids than study Holy Scripture. After a somewhat obscure comparison between a dumb girl ("tumme meide") and an unripe pear ("grüene birne," l. 445), the narrator breaks into a diatribe based on the trope of the horrors of the evil wife ("übel wîp"):

Selten wirt sînes leides rât
Der ein übel wîp gewunnen hât,
Wenne nie kein tier erger wart
Denne ein wîp von übeler art (ll. 447–50)

(Rarely does a man who has married an evil wife escape suffering. A bad wife is worse than an animal could ever be.)

In this passage he does not elaborate on what exactly constitutes an "übel wîp." The audience would have understood his reference, since the personage of the bad wife was ubiquitous in contemporary lore and literature. He supplies more details in the passage titled "Von einer Toerîn" (ll. 4125–60), where he states that an undesirable wife is a spoiled girl who will not tolerate discipline and will act contrary to what she is told:

Si wolte stên, hiez man si sitzen,
Hiez man si wachen, si wolte slâfen,
Wolte man si strâfen, si schrei wâfen,
Wenne si was mit zarte erzogen:
Des was der man mit ir betrogen. (ll. 4128–32)

(She wanted to stand when she was told to sit; when she was told to stay awake she wanted to sleep; if she was to be punished she yelled for help; whenever she was treated tenderly, her husband lived to regret it.)

I find the line "wolte man si strâfen, si schrei wâfen" particularly chilling. Is it the meaning of this verse that an ideal spouse would take a beating without crying? Yet, stoic acceptance of physical punishment might also be construed as "evil," as we will later see in the case of Der Stricker's "Eingemauerte Frau." The narrator follows up his example of the bad wife with praise for a good wife. He hyperbolically guarantees a long and blessed life to a happy, God-fearing couple. Again, he does not elaborate at this point on what exactly constitutes a good wife. The audience supposedly is already in possession of that knowledge.

Just like the other texts of conduct literature, *Der Renner* makes reference to the Arthurian cycle. Surprisingly, though, the narrator is not nearly as enamored with the Arthurian characters as, for instance, *Der Welsche Gast*. Instead, he even condemns the readers of fiction as being unwise:

Alsô sint bekant durch tiutschiu lant
Erec, Iwan und Tristrant,
Künic Ruother und her Parcifâl,

Wigalois, der grôzen schal
Hât bejaget und hôhen prîs:
Swer des geloubt, der ist unwîs. (ll. 1222–26)

(Thus, well known through German lands are Erec, Iwan, and Tristrant, King Ruother and Lord Parzival, Wigalois who earned great
reputation and praise: whosoever believes in this is unwise.)

He rejects all knightly activity as foolish and speaks out against jousting and other shows of heroic prowess. He devotes an entire passage, "Von
stechen," to the mocking of tournaments, asking his readers to tell him the
purpose of this unnecessarily injurious and murderous activity: "Waz sol
sôgetân übermuot?" (l. 11592). His attitude toward chivalric pursuits is dis-
missive, his criticism of knights' behavior scathing.

Hugo's narrator condemns the courtly world for being in competition
with the spiritual world. He juxtaposes courtly honor with "ewiger fröide"
and is convinced that the two are incompatible—a position not held by the
writers of romance or by other authors of conduct literature.

The admonitions in the passage about jousting are directed solely at men;
oddly, the text does not mention ladies who played the significant part of
spectator at tournaments. In another passage, however, he does condemn
unnecessary gawking and gazing, for both men and women:

kurzewîlen und turnieren,
zwirlitzen, verwen, unnütze klaffen,
schate schouwen und üm sich kaffen (ll. 11740–42)

(Amusements and tournaments, running around, coloring the face,
vain gossiping, watching shadows and gawking around)

Hugo's harsh condemnation of the pursuits of knighthood and Arthurian
adventures are rooted in his religious beliefs.[4] As an author he furthermore
frowned on fellow poets who squandered their God-given talent with the
invention of silly stories; his own lofty purpose in life was training his contemporaries in righteousness with his well-worded admonitions. He rejects
Thomasin's stance on the usefulness of fictional characters in training young
people. While *Der Welsche Gast* aimed to prepare young men and women
for polite society, for keeping with worldly order and customs, *Der Renner's*

concept of social order is more closely related to that of Der Stricker's work. Its understanding of order on earth is closely tied into the hope for what it repeatedly calls "ewige fröude" (eternal joy). The author's call for adhering to worldly law and order is grounded in his faith-based view of a purposeful life, not a pursuit of honor in the worldly sense. Honor is linked to the soul; "sêle und êre" is a pairing that often reoccurs in Hugo's writing.

Since Hugo considers courtliness an idle pursuit, his text does not contain advice on fine manners. He equates striving for worldly honor, extolled in both Arthurian literature and most conduct literature, with lasciviousness:

> Die durch êre und durch wollust
> In die êwigen verlust
> Sich êwiglichen senkent
> Und wênic dar an gedenkent,
> Daz lîp und guot, fröude und guft
> Sint als ein nebel und als ein tuft. (ll. 2605–10)

(Those who through pursuit of worldly honor and sensual pleasures sink forever, in an eternal loss, reflect little on the fact that the body and possessions, joy and wantonness are only like a mist and like a vapor.)

Hugo's narrator warns his listeners/readers to be mindful of the ephemeral nature of all earthly things—bodies, wealth, and honorable social standing—and to hold in very low regard that which the world considers valuable. He shakes his fist at all sinners—especially those guilty of what he considers the worst sin: "hôchfart" (arrogance).

While condemning unruly and critical female gazing, he also harshly judges men who, as a consequence of not knowing how to control their wives, lose faith in their own visual perception. Such blinded—in the Freudian sense "castrated"—men fail to see or take for truth what is right before their very eyes.[5] The text recounts the "maere" (story) of a woman who tricks her husband into disbelieving his own eyes, which saw her lover jumping out of the bedroom window. His wife tells him that what he really saw was a goat. The wife does not even bother with a plausible explanation for the unusual presence of a goat in her chamber. Yet, it is not the adulterous wife but the foolish husband who is condemned and mocked in the story. He is the one who allowed her to overrule his own perception and visual knowledge. It is clear that the narrator blames the male victim for becoming a laughingstock, losing the respect of every man and woman hearing the story. The motif of the blind, duped husband is also found in Gottfried von Strassburg's *Tristan*, when Isolde fools King Mark into believing in her faithfulness, in spite of all the visual evidence to the contrary. Of course, even a story about a foolish husband does not lack misogynous undertones. The wife might be clever, but she is also a cruel, deceitful cheat.

Hugo's narrator condemns both the female appropriation of the gaze and the male renunciation of the gaze, which he equates with imprudence and powerlessness. In general, he takes a skeptical stance toward visual perception and visual acquisition of knowledge. He quotes the patriarch Saint Augustine:

Dâ von sprach sant Augustîn
Ein vil merklich wörtelîn:
Daz ist geloube und anders niht,
Daz man geloube des man niht siht. (ll. 18791–95)

(About that, Saint Augustine spoke some memorable words: this is faith and only this, that one believes what one doesn't see.)

The quote refers to what occurred after the resurrection of Christ. Jesus talked to the doubting Thomas, the disciple who would only believe what he saw with his own eyes. The narrator clearly disapproves of Thomas's lack of faith. A good medieval citizen was guided by faith and by obedience to authority, not by his own judgment. This rule applied specifically to women, as they had more authorities above them.

3

"The woman behind the wall"

As we have seen in the previous chapters, some conduct writers take a critical stance toward the behavior of their contemporaries, while others condone generally accepted courtly conventions. Heinrich von Melk belongs to the former group. Like Hugo von Trimberg, Heinrich warns his readers of the dire consequences of improper and immoral conduct in his didactic morality poem *Von des todes gehugde*.[1]

Much like Hugo von Trimberg, Heinrich von Melk is chiefly concerned with the salvation of his readers' souls. Heinrich specifically deplores the lifestyle choices of the ostentatiously immoral members of the privileged class; he practices "Ständekritik," a biting condemnation of class-specific misbehavior. Neither Hugo nor Heinrich advocates a drastic change of the societal system as a whole, but each aims to improve the moral and ethical conduct of individuals and groups within the existing framework of authority.

In light of the pious substance of their works, it is noteworthy that neither of these authors was directly employed or consecrated by the church; both were "freelance writers." Their independence empowered them to emphatically include church leadership in their scathing critique of upper-class behavior.

We do not know for certain when Heinrich was born, but it is assumed that it was in the twelfth century. His status was that of a "Laienbruder," a lay brother, or "Nichtkleriker," a non-cleric (*Von des todes gehugde* 160).

However, scholars are not even certain of his name; he is often referred to as "der sogenannte Heinrich von Melk" (the so-called Heinrich of Melk). Besides the fact that Heinrich's broad thematic—heaven and hell—fit with the political and theological climate of around 1200, there are no definitive ties, connections, or evidence of reception that link his work to his supposed peers.

I have chosen the example of Heinrich's *Mahnrede*, or admonition speech, because Heinrich, like Hugo, addresses women and incorporates remarks on the female gaze into his argument, both as an example of inappropriate behavior and, more surprisingly, as a tool toward acquiring worldly and spiritual understanding.

Just like Hugo's text, Heinrich's *Mahnrede* considers "hochvart," also called "übermute"—pride—the worst of all sins: "der hohvertige man ist des tiuvels suon," he proclaims (l. 302; The proud man is the son of the devil). Steeped in the ubiquitous misogyny of his time, the narrator asserts that the female sex is most susceptible to this temptation: "si reichsent almaeiste an den weiben" (l. 317; Women are most afflicted with it).

A notable difference between Heinrich's admonitions and the writings of Hugo von Trimberg (the *Winsbeckin* author) and Thomasin von Zerclaere is that *Mahnrede* appears to reject courtliness; the text does not call its readers or listeners to adhere to prevailing modes of behavior. Heinrich is, instead, nostalgic; he yearns for a return to the old ways when everything was better. In a *laudatio temporis acti*, he laments how people have grown more and more wicked with each generation. Heinrich's sermon criticizes the status quo, which is further than ever removed from perfection. The text expresses sincere doubt that the contemporary social order corresponds to the God-given *ordo*:

> die reichen lebent mit schalle,
> die armen mit gesuche.
> daz vindet man andehaeinen buoche. (ll. 420–22)

(The mighty are living high off the hog, while the poor are reduced to begging; this is not found in Scripture.)

The narrator sincerely deplores the fact that the powerful are living in luxury while the poor are starving. He warns his listeners that such a system is not in alignment with the teaching of the church fathers. The narrator does not, however, advocate an overthrow of worldly authorities—far from it. If anything, he wants to strengthen the existent authorities and urges his listeners to obey them. Heinrich's text is more akin to a sermon than to conduct literature, but in medieval writing the difference between the two is sometimes hard to discern. After all, genre categories were superimposed on the works in question much later, in the early nineteenth century. In the Middle Ages, texts were not inserted into a literary register. The advice that the dead father gives his son in Heinrich's poem is not at all unlike the advice given by Thomasin or by the father character in *Der Winsbecke*, even though Heinrich's ultimate purpose was different; he advised his listeners on how to avoid hell, not how to be pleasant company.

The specific passage in the poem dealing with the female gaze begins in line 597. Here, the narrator addresses a noblewoman at the viewing of her deceased husband:

> Nu ginc dar, wip wolgetan
> unt schowe deinen lieben man
> unt nim vil vlaeizchlichen war
> wie sein antlutze sei gevar,
> wie sein schaeitel sei gerichtet,
> wie sein har sei geslichtet! (ll. 597–602)

> (Now, beautiful wife, why don't you walk over there to your beloved husband and gaze at him and look carefully at his face, at the part of his hair, at the way his hair is smoothed down!)

He addresses the widow with a compliment, "wolgetan," which, in its inappropriateness, sets the tone for the cynical speech that follows. With a steady refrain of the words "Nu sich"—now look!—he points to the decaying corpse of the once handsome knight. In an ironic and macabre top-to-toe catalogue starting at the part of the man's hair (*Scheitel*), working his way down to the feet, the narrator juxtaposes the charms that the living man possessed with the horrors of his lifeless, putrid flesh.

Catalogues of beautiful body parts usually serve to describe female bodies. According to Sarah Westphal, such catalogue descriptions are more than innocent pieces of medieval poetics. Insofar as they are reserved for women of high social standing, they witness the textual construction of gender as a class attribute ("Camilla" 237). If, as Westphal points out, the catalogue description generally constructs gender as a class attribute, how can we understand this passage featuring a male object? What happens to the gender of this knight who passed from beautiful to repulsive, from active to passive, from life to death? I think that our knight suffered not only death but also a gender change. By using the trope of the top-to-toe catalogue, the text genders the dead body female, or, according to Laqueur's gender continuum, sliding toward the female side of the spectrum.

Carol Clover, who researched gender representation in Norse sagas using Laqueur's theories, writes about a similar regendering of the Viking character Egil. Egil became less and less active toward the end of his life, changing from a bloodthirsty fighter to a toothless hearth dweller, the "innan stokk" often described as women's domain (Clover 363–87). In the case of Heinrich's knight, the regendering happens not through forced passivity of old age but through the inescapable passivity of death. The man, in spite of all his success in life, ends up a passive object both of his wife's diegetic eyes and the extra-diegetic gaze of the listener/reader of the text.

Oddly, Heinrich reserves his harshest judgment for the clothing and appearance of the dead man. He mockingly points to the modern cut of the beard: "Nu sich, wa ist daz chinne / mit dem niwen barthare?" (ll. 616–17; (Now, look what has become of the chin with the stylish beard?). The mention of the beard slightly complicates the theoretical considerations of the corpse's gender, since a beard is an exclusively male attribute. James Schultz observed that the beard features as the only unmistakable marker of a male body in medieval literature. Schultz argues that male and female bodies are barely distinguishable by gender and are marked by social class instead ("Bodies"). As a further complication of interpretations of character gendering, Heinrich's insistence on the beauty of the dead knight's legs is not a "feminizing" strategy: in high medieval courtly fashion, women's legs were never seen, but male legs in tights were customarily exposed.

Heinrich's text and its admonitions regarding the female gaze escape easy categorization. The narrator does not admonish a young girl tempted to immorality by gazing, as Hugo's text did. Nor is he concerned with the negative implications of female sexual gazing, as was the mother character in the *Winsbeckin* text. Heinrich's narrator repeatedly encourages the probing female gaze—nu sich!—now look!—as a means toward the acquisition of knowledge—knowledge of the nature of death, a kind of memento mori. Simultaneously, he criticizes the wife's past sensual and visual enjoyment of her handsome husband's body. I detect a hint of cruelty, of Schadenfreude, in the following passage:

> wa sint die fuze, da mit er gie
> hoefslichen mit den frowen?
> dem muse du diche nach schowen,
> wie die hosen stunden an dem baeine;
> die brouchent sich nu laeider chlaeine! (ll. 622–26)

> (Where are the feet with which he pranced around beside the ladies in such a courtly manner? How often you ogled him from behind, admiring how the tights hugged his legs; they are not so closely fitted now, are they!)

The narrator clearly intends to shock, to horrify both the widow and the reader/listener. He seems to relish the mention of the dreadful details. Not satisfied with merely pointing to the visual evidence, he engages the olfactory sense:

> nu schowe in an al enmitten:
> da ist er geblaet als ein segel.
> der boese smach unt der nebel
> der vert uz dem uber donen
> unt laet in unlange wonen
> mit samt dir uf der erde. (ll. 630–35)

> (Just look at his middle; he is inflated like a sail; foul stench and vapors are wafting out from under his shroud and won't allow him to dwell above ground with you much longer.)

The narrator notably insists on a description of the rather unpleasant odor of the decaying body. Even though the sense of smell is low in the hierarchy of human senses and is often overlooked due to the hegemony of sight, odors are of immense social significance. When the narrator of this poem remarks upon the stench of the dead knight, he is not simply stating an obvious and horrifying fact; he is also pronouncing a moral verdict. Just as courtly texts (which I will discuss in the following chapters) contain analogies between beauty, nobility, and goodness, the medieval mind linked odor to moral character. For instance, hagiographical literature contains numerous descriptions of the pleasant smell of saints, dead or alive. While a good person's fragrance is delightful, morally objectionable people emit a foul stench.

Heinrich's poem has often been dismissed as an unremarkable sermon treating only the most conventional theological themes of sin and mortality. Superficially read, the content is, indeed, unoriginal and offers little new insight. Past scholarly efforts concentrated on philological pursuits like localizing and dating the untitled manuscript or filling in details of the biography of the "so-called" Heinrich von Melk. In regard to this inquiry, however, *Von des todes gehugde* is unique and valuable because it presents two different approaches to the female gaze. The text condemns female sexual ogling while simultaneously encouraging female gazing—nu sich! now look!—as a means of acquiring wisdom. Unlike the "good" female gaze—that is, the Winnicottian gaze with its comforting effect on the male subject through evoking the "good-enough mother"—the inquisitive gaze serves only the gazing woman herself. The dead knight is neither encouraged nor flattered by his widow's probing look. Heinrich's narrator surprisingly pushes the lady to gain visual knowledge, which is, according to Irigaray, "the patriarchal mode of knowledge par excellence" (*Speculum* 423). The purpose of the widow's gaze is to increase her understanding of the workings of the material world. The narrator wants her to acquire the wisdom that will help her—or so he hopes—make appropriate choices in life. He encourages the female gaze as a critical agency. Granted, the main concern is with her soul and not with a change of her situation on earth. Nevertheless, one can argue that this text relates to women as human beings, not as functional links in patriarchal society. This is what makes *Von des todes gehugde* so extraordinary compared to other medieval male-authored religious texts.

Der Stricker is another medieval writer for whom the gaze is a means for women to gain knowledge of the divine world order and their role in it. Among a wealth of short texts composed by this author, I will discuss his didactic tale "Die Eingemauerte Frau" as an example of his approach to the socialization of women into the medieval patriarchal system.

Der Stricker is thought to have been employed directly in the service of the church, unlike Hugo and Heinrich. As far as we know, Der Stricker was extremely well educated in theology, law, and literature.[2] He expressed himself in a variety of genres, among them the humorous collection of adventures of *Der Pfaffe Amis*[3] and the Arthurian romance *Daniel von dem Blühenden Tal.*

Der Stricker is best known as a Middle High German writer of a form of didactic literature called "bîspel." The "example" is a short didactic story that illustrates and describes a situation and draws a moral lesson from it. The purpose of this literature was twofold: to educate and to entertain. Der Stricker's particular interest seemed to be marriage and the "Godly order" reflected in the relationship of holy matrimony.

Der Stricker's story of "Die eingemauerte Frau" is an illustration of what happened when a wife refused to behave with the orderly, God-ordained submission that medieval patriarchal culture demanded of her. This tale is not unique in its subject matter; stories of walled-up women have been part of Western folklore tradition since antiquity. Since there is no readily available English version of this text, I include my own line-by-line translation of "Die eingemauerte Frau" in the appendix.[4]

The first six lines of the poem summarize the main theme—a wife's duty is to obey her husband; his duty is to keep his wife humble.

Ein ritter tugende rîche
nam ein wîp êlîche.
dô wolde si ir willen hân
und des sînen niht begân.
daz mohte er niht erlîden
und hiez siz gar vermîden. (ll. 1–6)

(A highly virtuous knight took a woman in marriage, but she wanted to have her own way instead of obeying his will. He would not stand for it and told her to give up.)

The text unequivocally takes the side of the husband—the first line introduces him as a wonderful person possessing a wealth of virtues, "tugende rîche." The narrator sets him up from the start as the righteous half of the couple. The anonymous wife is introduced without adjectives; she is simply a "wîp." By challenging his claim to her obedience, the woman leaves the virtuous man no choice but to beat her into submission.

Even to readers familiar with the tradition of misogynist clerical writing, the cold and brutal introduction of "Die eingemauerte Frau" has a chilling effect. The precise conduct lesson the text is aiming to teach is all but unintelligible to a modern audience. Who was entertained, educated, and delighted by it?

In lines 12 and 13 the husband beats his "wîp" with his fist and puts in words how worthless an object she is—he compares her to an empty sack. He knocks her around so violently that he wears himself out and only stops when his arm aches too much to continue. The wife's resistance to her husband consists of survival—she has the amazing resilience not to die from his violent blows. Since she is still talking, her husband, dissatisfied with the educational results of corporal punishment, decides to enclose her in a brick structure.[5]

dô hiez er mûren ein gaden,
daz wart gemachet âne tür;
ein venster kêrte er her vür.
dâ wart si inne vermûret. (ll. 36–39)

(He then commanded that a brick enclosure be built without a door, but with an opening for a window. There, she was walled in.)

Once she is walled in, he orders her to watch and witness through a small window whatever happens in front of her prison. Within the brick walls the woman's eyes begin to function as a sort of camera, taking in, reflecting, recording life outside of the enclosure, processing it without being part of it. She remains forbidden to speak, to be heard, to exist in a visible way. Her futile attempts to rejoin life fail: her husband remains silent and appears to forget about her entirely. The woman eventually capitulates and loses all hope. When even her own relatives turn against her, her spirits sink so low that not even the demons want to inhabit her flesh and flee. She eventually lets go of her passive resistance and gives up. This new-found humility, the text teaches, finally allows her to become a vessel for the Holy Spirit.

The punishment for her transgression is a complete exclusion from what used to be her existence. The life that would have been hers, had she not disobeyed her husband, unscrolls before her gaze. The record of those events becomes inscribed onto her listening and watching persona and will later serve as a deterrent for other unruly wives. Yet, her husband will not grant her an active role in the conversion of other women, even though, or perhaps because, she deeply desires it. Her own subjective impression and learning remain irrelevant; she serves only as a recording device and a physical reminder, a living monument of her own abuse and punishment, of what can and will happen if a wife strays from the narrow path of marital subordination.

Miran Bozovic, in his article "The Man behind His Own Retina," writes, "the window we are looking through functions virtually as an eye" (166). The enclosure of the evil wife becomes a camera obscura; it reflects the natural world. The immured woman, however, is not gazing at the real world but at an artificial projection of what her life might be, her part being played by another woman. It is a staging, a theatrical production of her life, or what it should have been had she followed the rules.

The window frames and mediates vision. The enclosed woman is an observing subject, a spectator, while the husband and the rest of the household necessarily become her visual objects. Her agency in this process might account for the later suppression of her testimony and speech. She must, eventually, return to her status as the object; the information and experiences she gathered must not be known. The enclosure was not a sufficiently harsh punishment, since it did not rid her of a desire to actively participate in her world. In a sudden turn of events, the woman undergoes a pivotal conversion in which she begins taking matters into her own hands. Desiring absolution, she sends for a priest. She convinces him of her repentance with a long, eloquent speech and then recruits him to talk to her husband on her behalf. When her husband approaches her, she delivers another lengthy soliloquy; this time she includes an apology.

The husband's reaction to her conversion is central and sums up the moral of the story: "Daz ich an der husvrouwen rach, / des hat si got bekeret" (ll. 228–29; Because of the punishment I gave to my wife, God turned her around). The man of the house collaborated with God in fixing his wicked wife.

She has a relapse into disobedience when she refuses to leave the enclosure (l. 239); apparently, she erroneously assumed that she had a choice in the matter. When she eventually leaves her prison, she proposes a new type of penitence for herself: she wants wicked wives brought to her so she can assist in converting them, reminding them of their sacred obligation to submit. She maintains with confidence: "daz kan ich nu wol geschaffen" (l. 265; I am capable of doing this now). Her deeply serious intention of working constructively within the confines and in support of patriarchy is reiterated emphatically three times. And each time, her announcements meet with merriment and patronizing praise from the male as well as the female personages in her surroundings.

Speaking before the assembled guests, she talks at length about her plan and emphasizes its importance with biblical vocabulary, such as the word "waerliche" (verily) frequently used in the Sermon on the Mount. And in lines 382–85 we learn that, indeed, female wickedness disappeared in the part of the country where the previously enclosed woman lived.

> beide ir sünde und ir schande,
> die vermitens alsô sêre,
> daz ir übel und ir unêre
> vor vorhten alsô gar verswant (ll. 382–85)

(Both her sin and her shame served as strong deterrents so that their wickedness and their dishonor simply vanished because of fear.)

However—and this revelation exceeds the cruelty of her violent abuse and imprisonment—none of the improvements in the womenfolk's marital disposition were due to the lady's training and speaking efforts. Every last wife's conversion was affected by naked fear—they all wanted to avoid being beaten, locked up, starved, and ostracized. The battered and reprogrammed woman loomed large as a passive warning sign, a symbol of her husband's authority. Her transformation into an object is finally completed through her becoming a site of pilgrimage, a "heilictuom" (l. 393).

So, why was this female character not permitted to actively support patriarchy? Why was she first silenced and then turned into an object? The reason is that her self-confident behavior and her intelligent speeches exemplify female agency, influence, or even equality—all of which subversively undermine the system she was claiming to support. By anointing herself a preacher and a savior—both roles explicitly reserved for the men—she unwittingly made a mockery of the norms of medieval society. Such behavior endangered the status quo and could not be tolerated. This is the reason why she had to be violently "emasculated."

All the religious and courtly conduct writers whose texts were discussed in this and the previous chapters supported the medieval class system; they firmly believed patriarchal order to be God-given and sacrosanct.[6] The ontological basis for closely monitoring women's behavior in general and the female gaze in particular lies less in misogyny than in the intrinsic desire of the patriarchal system to sustain itself. In a strange way, the belief in female inferiority was nothing personal. Some of the writers of patriarchal, misogynous texts, for example, Martin Luther, reportedly had a loving marital relationship. The restriction of female gazing was just one of the mechanisms to uphold organized societal structure. Obviously, the origin of the practice of limiting and regulating the female gaze is found in the abject position of females in medieval society. A woman's free gazing in a potentially sexual context would have signaled noncompliance with God-given structures and might have led to a slew of unforeseeable negative consequences, such as the disturbance of the marriage or the inheritance system. Of course, there is a certain degree of circular reasoning involved in the creation of this patriarchal hierarchy. In the beginning of culture, women were considered weaker because of their smaller size and child-bearing function. Advanced societies built on that hierarchical foundation, since the exchange of women as the weaker element created bonds between men and thereby gave birth to culture (Lévi-Strauss explains these cultural origins in *The Elementary Structure of Kinship*). Hence, the patriarchal system developed, stabilized and ossified, supported by specific feedback loops that kept women in the inferior position by designating them inferior. They were considered inferior because they occupied this position. We have here a clear case of circular causality: A causes B and B causes A. One of the stabilizing feedback loops of the system was the control exercised over the female gaze. Felix Geyer and Johannes van der Zouwen write that "control is dispersed through the system" (83), which is proven, for example, by the fact that women were put in charge of the patriarchal education of younger women. Female gazing was appropriate as long as it functioned as a control mechanism of female behavior. Women themselves labored to support their own oppression.

4

"Ђe was as ђanдsome as ђe coulд be!"

MALE BEAUTY AND THE OGLING LADY IN THE *ENEASROMAN*

In the previous chapters we saw how premodern authorities attempted to regulate the way women looked at men. Worldly and religious writers alike aimed to contain female gazing within a rigid framework of patriarchal structures. Do not stare! and Do not be caught staring! are the emphatic commands of texts such as *Der Welsche Gast* and *Der Renner*.

Yet, the courtly romances, also composed in the High Middle Ages, are inhabited by a multitude of ogling ladies. These narratives have female characters who, against socially accepted norms, choose lovers based on visual attraction; male characters are objects of the female sexual gaze. These texts also feature examples of female characters who gaze "properly." The outcomes of these ladies' respective choices are drastically yet predictably different; the ideological substructures of romance literature and conduct literature are the same.

The first important female personage appearing in the *Eneasroman* is Queen Dido, whose history dates back to antiquity.[1] The medieval French adaptation *Roman d'Éneas*, written around 1160, is the source of Heinrich von Veldeke's version. Here, the tragic Dido personage is expanded in detail and importance; her character is devoid of the classical Dido's moral strength. Heinrich, however, includes a disclaimer regarding her failings— much like Isolde losing control of her life due to the effects of a magic potion, Dido falls victim to supernatural powers that force her to love Eneas; this detail provides a partial rehabilitation of her character.

The *Eneasroman* begins with a subtle reference to the female gaze in the description of how Dido seized power. After cleverly staking out a land claim through a ruse involving an animal skin,[2] Dido immediately begins construction on immense towers, taking up residence in one of the rooms with a view of the harbor.

> An einem ende uf dem mere
> hete frouwe Didô
> torne veste unde hô
> dâ ir wonunge was (ll. 401–4)

> (On the one side across the ocean Lady Dido owned solid and high towers where she resided.)

Dido, the mighty ruler of Carthage, knows the strategic advantage of watching over the sea access to her great city, of seeing a potential enemy before he invades. Curiously, there is no indication that Dido knew of the arrival of Eneas's ship in her harbor. She becomes aware of his presence only when Eneas's messengers make contact with her "in einer kemenâten" (l. 451)—an intimate space associated with female life or what the medievalist scholar Carol Clover identifies as "innan stokks" (385).[3] The location of first contact is a foreshadowing of another weakness: her inability to resist Eneas. Her guard was down from the beginning when she relinquished her strategic advantage of being able to "look ahead." Inexplicably, she gives the intruders the upper hand by allowing them to approach her without prior warning.

After the initial contact between Dido and the Trojan messengers, Eneas and his men ride into Carthage. They are watched from both sides of the street by noble ladies. The heroes are aware of their status as objects of the female gaze; they have carefully prepared themselves for just such an occasion. The text dwells in some detail on how the knights primped and prepped for their spectacular entrance:

> Dô wart her des ze râte,
> daz er alsô tâte,
> wande siz alle rieten
> dô hiez her gebieten

den rîtâren, die her wolde,
die her mit im fûren solde.
niht si dô ne beiten,
vil wol si sich gereiten
mit hêrlîchem gewande,
des si von ir lande
gnûch dare brahten (ll. 657–67)

(Then he decided to do what everyone had advised him to do. He assembled the knights whom he had selected to accompany him. They did not hesitate and dressed in luxurious clothes of which they had brought plenty from home.)

It is curious that the battle-worn soldiers traveled with their jewelry and their fancy outfits. After all, had they not departed under dreadful duress, fleeing their flaming fatherland, leaving behind their unburied dead? And yet they remembered to pack their party clothes:

zierheit maneger slahte
und manege grôze rîcheit.
dô si alle wâren gereit
sô ez hêren wol gezam,
Eneas zû ime nam
ritter funf hundert,
die hete her gesundert
unde erkoren ûz dem here
daz er braht het uber mere
die wâren ime alle gereit. (ll. 668–77)

(A great variety of jewelry, huge riches; when they were all decked out, befitting to noble lords, Eneas chose five hundred knights from the army that he had brought with him across the ocean; they were all at his service.)

This passage illuminates the importance for noblemen to look the part, especially in territory where their lineage was not general knowledge. Their attire undergirded the impressive statement made by their well-trained aristocratic bodies. Both body and clothes "made the man," as we also read in

Tristan: "Sîn wât und sîn figiure, / si schepfent wol an ime den man" (ll. 10856–57).

The description of the knights' flamboyant ride into Carthage and the details of their appearance paint a vivid picture, placing the reader in the observational spot, alongside the breathlessly ogling ladies. Naturally, the most beguiling fellow is the protagonist, Eneas.

> Eneâs der rîche
> der was ein schône man,
> deich û niht vollen sagen kan,
> wie rehte minnechlîche er was. (ll. 694–97)

(The noble Eneas was such a handsome man that I cannot fully express in words how truly lovely he was.)

The glowing review of his appearance notwithstanding, Eneas is not exactly a flawless hero. The text does not directly condemn him, but one has an uneasy feel about his showy, narcissistic arrival. He is, after all, a refugee who recently lost his position, his home, and his family. Where is his grief? What is worse, he cowardly runs away to save himself, avoiding a fight to the death. A good Germanic knight like Hildebrant in the *Hildebrantslied*, for example, would have rather died or even killed his own son than shrunk from armed confrontation. Numerous passages of male heroics can be found in the Norse sagas, where Vikings obstinately refuse to save their own lives and burn to death in their homes; even their wives proudly return into houses engulfed by blazing fires to join their mates. Eneas surely does not live up to their valiant example.

How did a second-rate hero like Eneas come to power in Troy in the first place? Quite easily—he married the daughter of the king: "des kuneges tohter was sîn wîb" (l. 39). The fair princess who helped him climb the Trojan social ladder is quickly forgotten. During Eneas's swift self-preserving exit after the fall of Troy (l. 140), an unidentified kidnapper carries her off. With ease, Eneas shrugs off responsibility and comments glibly: "ich ne weiz wer sime nam" (l. 142; I have no idea who took her). She is never mentioned again. Both the text and our hero suffer amnesia regarding the unceremonious disappearance of this poor lady.

Eneas's bravery is in doubt again when he fights Turnus; wearing a magical suit of armor, Eneas never faces real danger, unlike his opponent. Eneas has an additional ace up his sleeve: he stands under the special protection of the goddess Venus. And why wouldn't she keep him safe? She is, after all, his mother: "Venûs diu gotinne, / diu frowe is uber die minne, / wâre sîn mûder" (ll. 45–47). Venus continually keeps an eye on her son:

Do gesach sîn mûder Vênûs,
daz im der hêre Turnûs
gerne schaden wolde (ll. 5597–99)

(That's when his mother Venus saw that Lord Turnus was intending to hurt him.)

By virtue of his divine parentage, Eneas received a personal security alert from the gods to save his life and beats a hasty retreat across the ocean (ll. 55–58). When Eneas turns up in Carthage he is once again ready and willing to accept the help of another powerful woman—Dido. The narrator of Hartmann von Aue's adventure *Erec* criticizes Eneas's discourteous treatment of the queen:

über sê vuor von dan,
und wie er ze Kartâgô kam,
und wie in in ir genâde nam
diu riche vrouwe Dîdô,
unde wie er si dô
vil ungeselleclîchen liez
und enleiste ir niht des er gehiez:
sus wart diu vrouwe betrogen (*Erec* ll. 7555–62)

(He sailed across the ocean, and when he got to Carthage the powerful Lady Dido took him under her wings. He abandoned her and left her all alone and did not keep his promise to her; this is how the lady was betrayed.)

Eneas's good looks, not Dido's, are emphasized in the description of their initial encounter. The knight, however, is more infatuated with the material wealth of the city than with the lady's charms. He is taking visual possession of her domain. Dido, on the other hand, can't resist ogling the handsome Eneas; her lack of self-control, however, is less a reflection on his perfect bone structure than on the interference of his overprotective mother, Venus, and her other son, Cupid, who cast a love spell on Dido:

> Dô der hêre Enêas
> in die borch komen was
> frowen Dîdonen ze hûs,
> do geschûf sîn mûder Vênûs
> und sîn brûder Cupidô,
> daz in diu frouwe Dîdô
> starke minnen began (ll. 739–46)

(When Lord Eneas came to the city, to the castle of Lady Dido, his mother Venus and his brother Cupid caused Lady Dido to fall madly in love with him.)

Eneas seems at ease with some ladies looking after him and other ladies "looking him over." During his triumphant ride through the city he becomes the voyeuristic object of the female gaze—ladies ogle him with abandon and he doesn't seem to mind one bit:

> dô der mâre helt balt
> mit sînem volke dar în reit,
> die strâze vander vile breit
> und sach beidenthalben stân
> manich hûs wol getân
> und manich rîche palas,
> daz von marmore was,
> dâ her vor solde rîten,
> und gesach en beiden sîten
> magede unde frouwen,
> die in wolden schouwen (ll. 710–20)

(And as the brave and well-known hero rode into town with his men, he found a rather fine broad avenue before him; both sides of the road were lined with many beautiful houses and rich palaces built of marble, and he rode past them; and on both sides he saw young girls and ladies who wanted to look at him.)

Some medievalists—Helen Solterer, for example—argue that the female spectator's gaze is sexualized, but moral watchdogs do not disallow it, since it inspires the knight to greater achievement. The act of jousting, Solterer believes, might be viewed as a mating ritual performed for the viewing pleasure of the ladies. I find Solterer's theory that courtly ladies at tournaments gazed sexually with the approval of society problematic, to say the least. None of the textual evidence collected for my inquiry supports this idea. Instead, I believe that the ladies' gaze functions as a device for inclusion in a medieval social group. The ladies and their visual objects form a community. A sexual female gaze would have subverted, not supported, the all-important principle of orderly medieval society; it was not a woman's role to initiate mating with her gaze. When such a love connection did occur it was strongly condemned, both in conduct literature and, indirectly, through undesirable consequences, in the romances.

It is a fact, though, that the vision of male beauty as observed by female spectators is one of the major preoccupations of the *Eneasroman*.[4] Men are described as physically appealing far more frequently than women. One example is the list of all of Turnus's fighters, especially the description of Lausûs, "der schôniste jungelink, / den der ieman gesach" (ll. 5034–35). Here, the emphasis is put on "von manne und von wîbe" (among both men and women)—Lausûs has the best-looking body, eclipsing the prettiest ladies. I wonder, though, how the narrator might have compared male and female beauty to arrive at that judgment. Was Lausûs more slender and more delicately built than the ladies? Were his lips even redder and his skin even whiter? Sadly, the text doesn't divulge the criteria determining the winner of this gender-neutral beauty contest.

When Eneas makes his grand entrance into the city, the only beauty piercing his heart is that of the splendidly built monuments. The streets charm him with their ornate design and opulent palaces. His initial positive impression of the "borch" is confirmed; he is thrilled with the city's wealth and deems it worthy of his presence. He decides to take up residence there.

Dido, on the other hand, does not have the luxury of choosing between giving herself, body and soul, to this uninvited guest and offering standard hospitality services. Venus made up Dido's mind for her. After suffering a sleepless night, Dido confesses her "Liebesqual," her love torture, to her sister Ana, who also noticed that Eneas is rather good-looking:

> Ir sprechet von dem manne,
> den ich mit ougen nie gesach.
> sô ich mich verdenken mach,
> ir nis dehein sô wol getân,
> hern sî ein edel Troiân
> von hêreme geslehte (ll. 1536–41)

(You are talking about a man on whom I have never laid eyes. I think that no other is as handsome, unless perhaps another Trojan of noble descent.)

The first two lines of Ana's response are remarkable. With typical courtly hyperbole she claims what I interpret to mean: "I never before laid eyes on another man as gorgeous as he is." She goes on to praise his good looks, accepting them as proof of his noble descent. Here, the text draws on a rich premodern literary tradition of associating bodily beauty with noble or royal descent. In "Bodies That Don't Matter," James Schultz closely examined this connection between the body and nobility. He claims that in the medieval romance *Tristan* by Gottfried von Strassburg, male and female desirable bodies are similar; not gender but social class differentiates them. One's position in society shapes the exterior; this applies not only to dress or grooming but also to physiognomy, the skin and bones of the body. John Berger's research supports Schultz's theory of social class inscribed on bodies. He claims in *About Looking* that it is easy to identify men depicted in a photograph as peasants, even though—or especially because!—they are wearing clothes originally designed for a different social class. Physical labor molds and modifies the human body; it broadens shoulders, enlarges arms and hands, and influences posture and stride. A knight's body, then, was also shaped by the specific activities of the medieval ruling class, such as riding, hunting, sword fighting, and so forth. A contemporary could decode these visual cues to determine a man's social origin, whether he was dressed or naked.

Ana, Dido's sister, takes it a step further: Having gazed at Eneas's well-conditioned body, "her is scône und lussam" (l. 1545), she not only concludes that he springs from nobility but also assumes that he is morally superior, "frumech unde gût" (l. 1547). She has no facts on which to base her positive judgment. Dido and her people heard only one eyewitness tell of events surrounding the fall of Troy: Eneas himself. Oddly, he did not even embellish the story of how he ran away to save his own life. Dido barely listens to his speech, anyway. She devours him with her eyes while he speaks. "Sine rûchte waz her sprach, / wan daz her eht sprâche" (ll. 1234–35). The lovesick queen, nevertheless, seems surprised by Ana's glowing words about Eneas's character. She inquires: "War umbe lobet irn nû so?" (l. 1554; Why are you praising him thus?) Apparently, her infatuation has not yet progressed to the point of affecting all her critical thinking skills, but she is quickly falling under his spell.

The voyeuristic gaze directed at a human object was feared to exercise power over that person. One example of this notion is the dread of the evil eye, discussed in the introduction. Gazing universally signifies a psychological relationship of power in which the gazer dominates the object of the gaze. Ogling and staring at someone can be read as a form of aggression, perhaps even culminating in an offense punishable by law. Curiously, though, in Dido's case, her gaze exercises a destructive power, not over Eneas, but over herself. She is aware of it and, in a monologue, regretfully acknowledges the fact that her downfall started when she first laid eyes on Eneas:

Ouwê, hêre Enêas,
wie gewaldech ich was,
dô ich ûch êrst erkande
und gesach in diseme lande.
des mûz ich sêre engelden. (ll. 2355–61)

(Woe is me, Lord Eneas, how powerful I was when I met you, when I saw you for the first time in this land. I am definitely now paying the price for that.)

Eneas, the male object, the "victim," seems very little affected by the power of the gaze. He retains his strength, his integrity, and his decision-making ability while Dido progressively disintegrates; her social position as well as her physical and mental health collapse like a house of cards. It is as if the gaze—in particular, the desiring gaze—weakens and injures the female character—no matter whether she is the visual object or the gazing subject.[5]

Dido's gaze objectifies Eneas; she transgresses by appropriating the male gaze in the Freudian sense. Ann Kaplan, a feminist film theorist who asks the question of the gender of the gaze, tries to untangle the paradox by suggesting that the gaze is not necessarily male but that to own and activate the gaze is to be in the masculine position (*Feminism* 130). Dido usurps the masculine position, leading to her fall and ultimate death. Her appropriation of male powerful and sexual gazing potentially endangered the patriarchal order, in which women cannot be permitted to act upon their desires.

Eneas and Dido have one last encounter after her tragic death. He meets her in Hades, where he travels for a consultation with his late father. He finds him blissfully frolicking in the Elysian fields. Dido, in contrast, who committed the unforgivable sin of suicide, is stuck in a place with less frolicking and more gnashing of teeth. Eneas looks at her and feigns sympathy. This scene, of course, is reminiscent of the Orpheus story, retold in Ovid's *Metamorphoses*. Eneas, unlike Orpheus, did not go looking for his lover, but just happens to run into her in the underworld. While Orpheus eternally mourns the loss of his Eurydice, Eneas speedily recovers and promptly falls in love again, this time with the virginal princess Lavinia. Dido's ghost is well aware that her misery got started when she first laid eyes on Eneas. In Hades, she belatedly refuses to gaze at him.

> dâ mûste her erkennen
> froun Didônen die richen,
> diu sich sô jâmerlîchen
> dorch sînen willen hete erslagen.
> ir schaden wolder klagen,
> trûrechlîche sach hers an.
> mit dem houbet wankte si him dan,
> sine wolden niht ane sehen; (ll. 3296–3303)

(Then he also had to see the noble Lady Dido who had so shamefully taken her own life because of him. He wanted to mourn her loss and looked at her sadly. She turned her head away and did not want to look at him.)

While Dido's sensual gazing sets up her demise from the start, another important female character in the *Eneasroman* falls prey to the power of the desiring gaze: Camilla. This lady, however, is introduced not as a gazer but as a visual object. Her body is scrutinized as if she were a knight, "als ein jungelink" (l. 5191). Camilla is an androgynous figure, a female soldier, an Amazon. Her status as a virgin is emphatically underlined, since a rejection of her female sexuality is a necessary precondition for her position as a fighter. When Camilla rides into town to join the army of her friend Turnus she becomes the object of the gaze, much like Eneas on his ride to Carthage.

> dorch Laurente sie reit
> Camille diu rîche
> vil behagelîche.
> die hêren und die frouwen,
> die si wolden schouwen,
> si quâmen zû den strâzen,
> si stunden unde sâzen,
> ze den venstern si lâgen.
> alle die si gesâgen,
> die dûhte si vil wol getân (ll. 5290–99)

(She rode through Laurentum, the powerful and proud Camilla. Lords and ladies who wanted to see her came to the streets. They stood around, they sat there, they leaned out of their windows. All who saw her thought that she was utterly stunning.)

Not only is Camilla beautiful, but she is aware of her role as the object of the public gaze. Here, the ubiquitous rhyme "frouwen . . . schouwen"—for once!—refers to a female object.

But this busy battle-hardened warrior maiden has little in common with a stationary work of art. Most importantly, her male onlookers might find an encounter with her to be rather deadly. She doesn't use a girly weapon, either, but kills in a masculine, bloody fashion—she forcefully penetrates her enemies' bodies with a sword: "dorch den lîb si in stach" (l. 9010). And again: "Kamille den andern stach, / daz her tôt viel ûf daz gras" (ll. 9026–27)

Another gender reversal occurs when Camilla is intently ogled during her martial activities, just like the other soldiers who happen to be male. A cowardly little knight named Arras engages in voyeuristic pursuit of her without daring to come too close. He understandably fears for his life after observing her knightly prowess:

> do was einer der hiez Arras
> mit den Troiâren dâ.
> Kamillen reit her allez nâ
> verre allen den tach.
> der markte unde sach,
> wie si slûch und wie si stach
> und wie sie ir spere brach
> und wie sie justierde
> und wie sie pungierde
> und wie ritterlîch si slûch:
> want des tete sie genûch
> unglîch einem wîbe. (ll. 9046–57)

(There was one with the Trojans whose name was Arras. He had followed Camilla all day, keeping his distance. He noticed and he saw how she hit, pierced, and split her lances, how she held up in duels and battles, how courageously she fought. She behaved like a true knight, not like a woman.)

Camilla is oblivious to the fact that she is Arras's voyeuristic object: "don nam frowe Kamille / neheiner slahte ware des" (ll. 9062–63). She lacks Eneas's narcissism and does not put on a show. Only when Camilla sees the stunning helmet of Chloreus, the Trojan priest, does her status shift from desired object to desiring subject. The account of the richly decorated helmet resembles the description of Camilla's own impressive appearance. After she killed the wearer of the desirable helmet, she herself is stabbed by her Trojan voyeur, the cowardly Arras, who had been watching her passionate pursuit from a distance. Once again, the desiring female gaze is harshly punished. Camilla had remained successful throughout her splendid martial career until she began casting desiring glances on an awesome piece of headgear.

While the battle between Trojans and Italians rages on, another woman, the young Lavinia, becomes Venus's next target. The goddess—usually known for passions other than mothering—once again takes up her son Eneas's case and strong-arms the king's daughter into falling in love. Granted, the teenager liked what she saw before Venus's arrow ever hit her. She gazes out of her window and sees a knight who could not possibly be any more handsome. Furthermore, since his reputation had preceded him, she was already infatuated with the "idea" of Eneas before she ever laid eyes on him.

> dô sach diu junkfrowe her abe
> von dem venster dâ si lach.
> den hêren sie wol besach,
> den minnesâlegen Troiân.
> wie wart her ie sô wol getân,
> hern mohte niemer schôner sîn!
> daz hete ouch daz magedîn
> dâ bevor vil wol vernomen.
> dô her dô dare was komen,
> do gesach sie die wârheit. (ll. 10020–29)

(There, the young girl looked down from the window where she perched. She looked at him very closely, the gorgeous Trojan. He was as handsome as he could be! She had already heard rumors about his good looks, and now that he was here she could see that it was all true.)

Again, it is the knight's body that becomes the object of the gaze and hence the object of desire. His good looks, not hers, are the catalyst for love. Mother Venus, not willing to take any chances, reinforces Lavinia's infatuation with a magic arrow.

> Dô der hêre dare quam
> und sîn diu maget lussam

dâ nidene wart gewar
und si ir ougen kêrde dar,
dâ si was ûf deme hûs:
dô schôz si frouwe Vênûs
mit einer scharphen strâle. (ll. 10031–37)

(When the knight arrived and the girl saw him down there, when she gazed at him from her space in the castle, Lady Venus shot her with a sharp arrow.)

Lavinia bears witness to Eneas's arrival in much the same way other courtly ladies did during his triumphant ride into Carthage. In both situations the ladies are the active gazers while Eneas is the passive object of the gaze. The female onlookers hold a privileged position, since their gaze is focused on their object, yet they are not looked at, at least not with the same intensity and scrutiny. Ogling men was, apparently, a common female diversion. Lavinia, for example, admits that she often indulged in knight-gazing: "Ich hân vil dicke gesehen / manegen wol getânen man" (ll. 10176–77; Often enough I have seen so many handsome men); fortunately for Eneas and, ultimately, the city of Rome, her previous ogling pursuit never caused her to fall in love. Lavinia has the advantage of not only perceiving Eneas first but of already having heard of him before she sees him for the first time.[6]

Lavinia's young heart was ripe and ready for love, tenderized by the heroic tales circulating around the figure of Eneas as well as by the facts of life she just learned from her mother. Ironically, it is precisely this infatuation with Eneas that the queen tried to prevent with her educational talk. Her political aspirations demanded an alliance with Turnus, to whom she would give her daughter to validate and cement the pact. But, even though giving a daughter in marriage to bring about political goals was common for male rulers, the queen's image suffered substantially from her patriarchal, unladylike wheeling and dealing.

The queen's transgression of making political choices without her husband's blessing has dire consequences for her. She is condemned to an existence as a two-dimensional caricature failing to reach her goals and reaping the disrespect of everyone, including her husband and daughter. She eventually fades out of the narrative, pathetically withering away like a neglected house plant.

As far as the effectiveness of her "sex talk" is concerned, the queen could not compete with Venus's determination to pave the way for her son's ascent to power. Lavinia has no choice: "sô daz si mûste minnen, / si wolde oder enwolde" (ll. 10041–42; so that she had to love him, whether she wanted to or not).

After being hit by Venus's arrow, Lavinia endures the same love torture that Dido suffered. Lavinia expresses herself in a long "Minnemonolog" stretching over 435 verses. Her love for Eneas, as far as she can tell, started when she first saw him. She gushes over his good looks and wonders what would happen if other women saw him. Would they also love him?

Wie wart her ie sô wol getân,
sin houbet und aller sîn lîb!
ichn wiz ob in alliu wîb
also minnen die in gesehen. (ll. 10102–5)

(How handsome he is, both by face and body! I don't know if it is only me or if all women fall in love with him when they see him.)

The detailed description of the psychological process occurring after she sees Eneas is divided into four parts. First, Lavinia directs her desiring gaze at him and is inflamed by love. Second, she becomes aware of her own attraction to him, partially based on the good opinions—curiously also related to beauty—she heard from others. Third, Lavinia logically concludes that if his appearance had this effect on her, it might have the same effect on other women, and she decides to dismiss this disconcerting thought. Fourth and last, in a brief moment of lucidity, Lavinia regrets that she laid eyes on Eneas: "Mir is leit daz ich in ie gesach" (ll. 10108). But it is too late; love has entered Lavinia by way of her eyes. The image of handsome Eneas penetrated her heart like it did Dido's, without either one of them in a position to prevent it.[7]

When Lavinia and Eneas finally discover that their love is mutual, Lavinia's gazing follows the classic trajectory: she looks down to him from her elevated chamber, admiringly and lovingly, observing his uneven fight with Turnus (who lacks a magic suit of armor):

dô was diu maget Lavîne
ûf ein palas vile hô
und sach daz man ez schûf alsô,
daz si dâ vehten solden
die si beide haben wolden (ll. 12208–12)

(The maiden Lavinia was looking down from a very high building and saw that preparations were being made for a fight between her two suitors.)

Things are finally back to normal. Lavinia is the desirable object of two men, and her gaze on Eneas is neither lustful nor critical; it is the idealizing, loving motherly gaze. It is nonthreatening, supportive, and entirely free of the threat of castration.

Heinrich von Veldeke's version of the Eneas story represents beauty as a predominantly male trait, while the action of ogling handsome bodies is associated with female characters. Women, it turns out, are the oglers, not the oglees. Interestingly, when the ability to see or to foresee is lost, the power associated with the gaze is also lost. In any case, the female gazer's voyeuristic pleasure remains short-lived—she will not profit from her fleeting position of power over the knight whom she chose as the object of her gaze.

Five illustrations from the Codex Manesse, dated to the first third of the fourteenth century, reproduced courtesy of the University of Heidelberg Library. (Digital reproductions of the Codex Manesse illustrations are available online at the University of Heidelberg Library, http://diglit.ub.uni-heidelberg.de/diglit/cpg848/.)

•

Fol. 11v "Herzog Heinrich von Breslau." The knight and poet, Duke Henry of Breslau, is handed a wreath by one of four admiring ladies. Their hand gestures symbolize lively conversation.

Fol. 17r "Der Herzog von Anhalt." Four similar-looking ladies observe beautifully adorned knights, among them Henry I, during a tournament.

Fol. 43v "Graf Wernher von Homberg." This miniature shows the martial exploits of the Swiss poet Count Wernher of Homberg, closely watched by ladies behind the crenellations.

Fol. 46v "Herr Jakob von Warte." Lord Jakob of Warte has the help of four ladies while taking a bath. Three of them are watching him closely, while the fourth is tending to the fire heating his bathwater.

Fol. 52r "Herr Walther von Klingen." Five ogling ladies fawn over the poet and knight Walther of Klingen during a tournament.

5

"The most handsome knight that ever lived"

FEMALE SCOPOPHILIA IN *PARZIVAL*

To this day, more than eighty manuscripts of Wolfram von Eschenbach's *Parzival* remain, proving that this text was immensely popular and widely read in the Middle Ages. In the following pages I examine how the representation of the female gaze in this poetic work affects the trajectory of the plot and simultaneously lends support to contemporary teachings on appropriate female behavior.

Right from the beginning, the narrative is driven by the desiring gaze of a female character. Gahmuret, Parzival's father, arrives in the fictional empire of Zazamanc, where he enjoys the hospitality of Queen Belakane:

> der küneginne rîche
> ir ougen vuocten hôhen pîn,
> dô si gesach den Anschevîn.
> der was sô minneclîche gevar,
> daz er entslôz ir herze gar,
> ez waere ir liep oder leit:
> daz bezlôz dâ vor ir wîpheit (stanza 23: ll. 22–28)

(When the powerful queen laid eyes on the knight from Anjou, a strong desire welled up in her. He was so lovely that her heart opened up for him, for better or for worse, even though female shyness had kept it closed until now).[1]

The situation is similar to the meeting of Dido and Eneas in Veldeke's *Eneasroman*: in both cases, a powerful female ruler welcomes an impoverished hero to her domain and instantly falls in love with him. When she beholds the handsome knight, this formerly chaste queen is inflamed with lust. Gahmuret knows his effect on the female desiring gaze; he elaborately prepared for their first meeting:

> balde wart dô Gahmurete
> rîchiu cleider dar getragen:
> diu leite er an. sus hôrte ich sagen,
> daz diu tiure waeren.
> anker die swaeren
> von arâbischem golde
> wârn drûfe alse er wolde. (stanza 22: l. 30; stanza 23: ll. 1–6)

(Very soon Gahmuret was supplied with beautiful garments which he put on. I heard that they were quite expensive. He even commanded that they bring anchors of heavy Arabian gold.)

Gahmuret, like Eneas, is virtually destitute. As the second son of a noble family he is not an heir and depends on the largesse of his gracious hostess. Gahmuret's deck is not stacked in his favor by having the goddess of love as his mother, and he has to work a little harder than Eneas. He succeeds, nonetheless: "ir ougen dem herzen sân / daz er waere wol getân" (stanza 29: ll. 1–2; Her eyes told her heart that he was handsome). She gives in to her desire.

> dô pflac diu küneginne
> einer werden süezer minne,
> und Gahmuret ir herzen trût (stanza 44: ll. 27–29)

(The queen and her beloved Gahmuret enjoyed each other's sweet love.)

A female personage—even one as powerful as Queen Belakane—who lets her eyes wander and who lusts after a handsome foreign soldier will suffer the consequences of her inappropriate behavior. For Dido, the cost of her fling with Eneas is loss of honor, self-respect, and, ultimately, life. Belakane's fate is equally disastrous, if not more so than Dido's. While Eneas heavy-heartedly leaves Dido because his destiny demands it, Gahmuret abandons his wife out of boredom:

dâ was der stolze küene man,
unz er sich vaste senen began.
daz er niht ritterschefte vant,
des was sîn vröude sorgen pfant. (stanza 54: ll. 17–28)

(The proud and brave knight stayed, until he was overcome with such
a longing for adventures that it consumed all his joy.)

He sneaks off in the middle of the night without bidding her adieu, taking several of her prized possessions and leaving behind nothing but a short
note and his unborn offspring.

When the boy is born, he has checkered skin which the text attributes
to his mixed race. The devoted Belakane loves her baby's white spots more
because they remind her of her husband. The queen hopes for his return,
but he has moved on; he is attracting the female desiring gaze elsewhere.

Back west, Gahmuret not only elevates himself by assuming the title
of king; he also prances around wearing the helmet and armor he stole
from Belakane's treasury right before he clandestinely and unchivalrously
departed. At the tournament of Kanvoleis, everyone's gaze is fixed on this
richly decorated knight who outshines the competition. The luster of his
armor is so intense that looking directly at it can be hazardous to one's
health:

er schein als ob hie brünne
bî der naht ein queckez viur.
verblichen varwe was im tiur:
sîn glast die blicke niht vermeit:
ein boesez ouge sich dran versneit. (stanza 71: ll. 12–16)

(It gleamed like a lively fire in the night; there wasn't a single dull spot.
Its glow attracted all the looks; it was so strong that it might have even
hurt weak eyes.)

According to this passage, the sparkly attire is the main attraction, while
the man Gahmuret features as the lesser dish of the visual feast. However,
Gahmuret has serious competition at the tournament of Kanvoleis as the
object of female gazing. The king of Gascogne is also easy on the eyes:

daz vorder teil des grîfen hie
der künec von Gascône truoc
ûf dem schilt, ein ritter cluoc.
gezimieret was sîn lîp
sô wol geprüeven kunnen wîp. (stanza 72: ll. 24–28)

(The front part of the eagle was carried by the king of Gascogne, as a
coat of armor on his shield. He was so handsomely adorned that he
definitely passed muster among the watching ladies.)

Surprisingly, neither the ogling ladies nor Gahmuret himself cares that
he is married. Herzeloyde, the virginal queen, openly pursues him, sneaking
into his tent to catch a glimpse:

diu küngîn an die snüere reit
mit manger werden vrouwen:
si wolte gerne schouwen
den werden künec von Zazamanc. (stanza 82: l. 30; stanza 83: ll. 1–3)

(The queen rode to the tent, accompanied by her pretty ladies in waiting; she so much wanted to see the handsome king of Zazamanc face
to face.)

She was not disappointed and loved what she saw: "er geviel ir wol, dô
si in ersach" (stanza 83: l. 11). The text makes it clear that it is the lady who
chooses the knight; the queen falls in love with the married king, not the
other way around. To be sure, he does not exactly discourage the advances
of the much younger queen. He waits until their second encounter to finally
confess to her that he is already married: "Vrouwe, ich hân ein wîp: / diu ist
mir lieber danne der lîp" (stanza 94: ll. 5, 6; Lady, I already have a wife and
I love her more than life itself). Herzeloyde is unfazed by his belated and
halfhearted pledge of marital fidelity—obviously, she was well aware of his
marital status when she began pursuing him. She gives him a frank answer:

Ir sult die moerinne
lân durch mîne minne.
des toufes segen hât bezzer craft.
nu ânet iuch der heidenschaft,

und minnet mich nâch unser ê:
wan mir ist nâch iuwerre minne wê. (stanza 94: ll. 11–16)

(My love should make you forget that dark-skinned woman. The blessing of baptism has the greater power. Just get rid of those heathen ways
and love me according to our laws because I am aching for your love.)

Soon enough, the reader learns that the ultimate outcome for the lady
is negative, after all. Herzeloyde's happiness with Gahmuret is brief: he dies
while she is expecting their first child. Even though Gahmuret is blessed
with a hero's battle death, he does not get off scot-free: he misses out on
a Christian burial. His remains are interred on pagan ground in Bagdad,
which, for medieval Christians, amounted to a rather severe punishment.

In the meantime, Herzeloyde derives joy from her baby, whom she considers a reincarnation of Gahmuret:

ich was vil junger danne er,
und bin sîn muoter und sîn wîp.
ich trage alhie doch sînen lîp
und sînes verhes sâmen. (stanza 109: ll. 24–27)

(Even though I was much younger than he, I became his mother and
his wife since I am carrying his life and his seed within me.)

Herzeloyde turns her son into a source of sensual pleasure. She indulges
her voyeuristic tendencies by gazing at her naked infant:

dô diu küngîn sich versan
und ir kindel wider ze ir gewan,
si und ander vrouwen
begunden betalle schouwen
zwischen den beinen sîn visellîn.
er muose vil getriutet sîn,
do er hete manlîchiu lit. (stanza 112: ll. 21–27)

(After the queen had recovered and her infant was brought to her, the
other ladies joined her in looking at the little penis between his legs.
He was caressed a great deal because he looked just like a little man.)

Herzeloyde's devotion to her son was extraordinary in the light of contemporary customs. Barbara Newman writes that medieval noblewomen, probably in an effort not to get too attached—infant mortality was high—did not devote much time to their young children. Infants were handed over to wet nurses shortly after their birth (*Virile Woman* 94). Herzeloyde, in her excessive love for Parzival, did not entrust him to a nurse but nursed him herself. Herzeloyde's rejection of socially accepted, normal child-rearing practices, the text implies, led to his later difficulties in relating to his peers.

Herzeloyde puts Parzival in a difficult spot. She misses Gahmuret and tries to turn her son into a duplicate, a stand-in for his father. Breast-feeding Parzival reminds her of lovemaking with Gahmuret:

Diu küngîn nam dô sunder twâl
diu rôten välwelohten mâl:
ich meine ir tüttels gränsel:
daz schoup si im in sîn vlänsel.
selbe was sîn amme
diu in truoc in ir wamme:
an ir brüste si in zôch,
die wîbes missewende vlôch
si dûht, si hete Gahmureten
wider an ir arm erbeten. (stanza 113: ll. 5–14)

(The queen eagerly took her red points, I am talking about her nipples, and shoved them in his little mouth. She who had carried him in her womb was also his wet nurse. She pulled him to her breasts, untouched by unwomanly nature, and almost felt like, once again, she was holding Gahmuret in her arms.)

The references to her breasts and her womb, incidentally, are echoes of Mariolatry; this association was common throughout medieval texts. But Herzeloyde is a flawed, problematic Mary-figure. While treating Parzival as a reincarnation of his father, she selfishly shelters the boy from finding out about his lineage. She does not even tell him his own name, nor does she talk to him about his father's knightly fame—a terrible omission in the light of the medieval concept of heroism, immortalized in the Old High German poem *Hildebrantslied*. By severing the link between Parzival and his father, Herzeloyde does a grievous injustice to both of them.

Motherly affection and selfish desire intersect in Queen Herzeloyde's behavior toward Parzival. Was it maternal love that caused her to sacrifice a life at court, or was it possessiveness? The same dichotomy exists in her gaze directed at Parzival: is it pleasure-seeking and sexual, or nurturing and motherly? In the end, Herzeloyde did not overstep the boundaries of her world with impunity. All her scheming and planning failed; she loses her son. In a desperate attempt to keep Parzival from joining the Arthurian court, she dresses him in ridiculous clothes, trying to destroy his advantage as a beautiful object of the gaze (stanza 127). In an attempt to make his noble origins illegible, she covers up the signs of high birth visibly inscribed on his body.

When Parzival leaves her, Herzeloyde dies the poetic death of a broken heart. Or, more precisely, she dies from "gaze withdrawal":

> dô si ir sun niht langer sach
> (der reit enwec, wem ist deste baz?),
> dô viel diu vrouwe valsches laz
> ûf die erde, aldâ si jâmer sneit
> sô daz si ein sterben niht vermeit. (stanza 128: ll. 18–22)

(When she could not see her son, who rode off cheerfully, any longer, the good lady sank to the ground with a broken heart and death snatched her away.)

The motherly gaze of Herzeloyde built up and nurtured Parzival, but it also sustained Herzeloyde herself; when the object of her gaze disappeared from sight, she lost her lifeline.

After being ogled exclusively by his mother and her small court while growing up in the woods, Parzival's beautiful body now entices a larger viewership. In his first meeting with the outside world, the knights scrutinize him carefully:

> von den helden er geschouwet wart:
> Dô lac diu gotes kunst an im.
> von der âventiure ich daz nim,

diu mich mit wârheit des beschiet.
nie mannes varwe baz geriet
vor im sît Adâmes zît.
des wart sîn lop von wîben wît. (stanza 123: ll. 12–18)

(The knights looked him up and down, and indeed he bore the marks of God's own handiwork. I have it from my source, which told me the truth of the matter, that from Adam's day till then none turned out better for looks than he, so that women praised him far and wide.)[2]

This passage describes a group of male viewers in the act of ogling a male body. It is remarkable how the narrator attempts to distract us from the "male-male" ogling by inserting the commentary that Parzival's beauty was praised "by women," even though the scene contains no gazing female characters. In *Between Men*, Eve Kosofsky Sedgwick explains this strategy in her theory of obligatory heterosexuality. Homophobia is an integral part of patriarchy, which depends on the exchange of women. Homosocial desire is masked by inserting women as connecting links between men. Women mediate the relationship of unacknowledged desire between men.

Kathleen Coyne Kelly also offers some useful thoughts about male gaze on male bodies in her article "Malory's Body Chivalric." She takes issue with the classic Freudian and Mulveyan formulation in which "men looking at men" is theorized as identification. She argues that, instead of automatic identification, a regendering of the object of the gaze is taking place. Kelly suggests that in theorizing the gaze we ought to move out of the rigid binary division of gender and into a more flexible system where subjects move along a scale of possible positions within an ideological matrix. She refers to the gender continuum theory of Thomas Laqueur, who maintains that sex before the seventeenth century was a sociological, not an ontological category (58).

These gender theories are useful for an alternate reading of Parzival's meeting with the knights. The boy is, indeed, a sexual object of the diegetic gaze of the soldiers, but he is more than that. The male gaze focuses on Parzival as a mode of class identification. Noble birth, in the Arthurian world, is part of nature and a stable referent. With their approving gaze, the knights initiate him into their circle.[3]

Parzival's second encounter with the outside world leads to his assault and robbery of Jeschute, whom the narrator describes in a top-to-toe catalogue of body parts: lips, teeth, hips, arms, and hands. Parzival is ignorant of both her beauty and the severe transgression he commits by invading her tent. He foolishly follows his mother's generic advice without thinking about its proper application. At this point in his development he is completely devoid of discernment.

Jeschute's judgment appears impaired, as well. Upon return of her husband to the crime scene, she mentions the beauty of Parzival:

dâ kom ein tôr her zuo geriten:
swaz ich liute erkennet hân,
ichne gesach nie lîp sô wol getân. (stanza 133: ll. 16–18)

(A fool came riding by. Of all the men I have seen in my life, he was the best-looking one.)

The fact that Jeschute praises Parzival's looks, elevating him above her husband, explains his wrath and her subsequent punishment. She forgot that the courtly lady's prime responsibility is the adoring gaze directed exclusively at her own knightly protector. Symbolically, her wandering eyes suffer, as well; they are turned red: "und iuwern ougen machen roete kunt" (stanza 136: l. 6).

When Parzival continues on his way, his status as a desirable object of the gaze is reconfirmed by a fisherman. After verifying that Parzival can pay for his overnight stay, the fisherman claims that he will assist the young man because of his good looks:

"diz tuon ich," sprach der vilân.
"ichne gesach nie lîp sô wol getân.
ich bringe dich durch wunder
vür des küniges tavelrunder." (stanza 143: ll. 11–14)

("I will do it," the peasant said, "because I have never seen anyone as good-looking as you are. I will take you to the king's round table because I am curious to know what's going to happen next.")

Why would the peasant be so eager to take Parzival to Arthur, except for receiving a monetary reward? A partial answer is found in the translation of "durch wunder," which I translated as "because I am curious to know." The fisherman knows of Arthur's court's lookism and is interested to see everyone's reaction to Parzival's beauty. The peasant realizes that this fellow represents an enigma—how can a poorly dressed country boy have the body of a nobleman?—and he is eager to watch the court solve this riddle. Nevertheless, the fisherman's curiosity remains unsatisfied. Shortly before he and his attractive protégé reach their destination, the fisherman suddenly remembers that his own shabby appearance would offend the beautiful people. When Parzival naively requests that he should accompany him further, the fisherman replies emphatically:

> diu mässenîe ist sölher art.
> genaeht ir immer vilân,
> daz waer vil sêre missetân. (stanza 144: ll. 14–16)

(Courtly society would very much disapprove if a simple man like me came too close.)

Once Parzival arrives at court, the next personage who feasts his eyes on him is, again, male. The knight Ither launches into a gushing laudatio, a trope of medieval literature, of the young man's beauty:

> "gêret sî dîn süezer lîp:
> dich brâht zer werlde ein reine wîp.
> ôwol der muoter diu dich bar!
> ichne gesach nie lîp sô wol gevar.
> du bist der wâren minne blic,
> ir schumpfentiure unde ir sic . . ." (stanza 146: ll. 5–10)

("Praised be your beauty. An excellent woman brought you into this world. Blessed be the mother that gave birth to you. I never saw anyone as handsome as you. You are the true vision of love, her defeat and her victory . . .")

The homage Ither pays to Parzival has religious overtones. He knows nothing about the young man's character, but he praises him as a gift from God. His exclamations are reminiscent of the "Hail Mary" in the biblical account. Ither praises the mother of Parzival and pronounces her blessed, again basing his moral judgment solely on Parzival's appearance.

Arthur's court sees Parzival and identifies him as one of their own, a member of their social group, the "brotherhood of knights." They are, of course, correct in their assessment: Parzival is, indeed, the son of one of their peers. Herzeloyde's ruse to keep him excluded through anonymity and the wrong clothing failed—his fellow noblemen see right through the feeble disguise. The gaze of the knights resting on the boy has one primary signifi- cance and communicates to him: You, Parzival, are part of us. You may need some work, but we accept you. The foundation for socialization of an indi- vidual, for creating the sense of belonging vital for the functioning of any social system, is contained in this gaze. This community-building quality is emphasized by the statement "im kunde niemen vîent sîn" (stanza 149: l. 1; Nobody could be his enemy). Arthur's queen also joins in Parzival's positive reception—she ogles him with pleasure, like everyone else: "do besach in ouch diu künegîn" (l. 2).

One person, however, is less than thrilled with Parzival's appearance at court: Sir Key. He cynically encourages the newcomer to engage in a duel with the seasoned fighter Ivreiz. Key is displeased with Parzival's arrival because he disturbs the order that Key is trying to preserve. Key hopes to get rid of him as quickly as possible. He simply cannot see past Parzival's uncourtly attire, and he is equally blind in regard to one of the essential ele- ments of the courtly system: female spectatorship. The importance of the female gaze completely escapes Key:

> sol iemen bringen uns den kopf,
> hie helt diu geisel, dort der topf:
> lât daz kint in umbe trîben:
> sô lobt manz vor den wîben.
> ez muoz noch dicke bâgen
> und sölhe schanze wâgen. (stanza 150: ll. 15–20)

(Somebody has to bring back the cup; here is the whip and there the top. Let the child whip it around so that the onlooking women can sing his praises. It won't be the last challenge he will have to face.)

Key likens Parzival's impending duel with the older knight to child's play amusing the ladies. He takes issue with the ogling ladies' role in male fight- ing, implying that the killing happens because of them in the first place. The narrator of *Parzival* expresses his criticism of chivalry in these passages, using Key as his mouthpiece.

To everyone's shock, young Parzival murders his cousin Ither during their brief, anticlimactic confrontation, for the sole reason of wanting to look like him. He kills him—and this is the worst part—by piercing through his eye with a javelin, a primitive, unchivalrous weapon. Parzival's unmitigated and unrestrained desiring gaze results in murder. The new favorite object of the female gaze kills the old one. Trevrizent, talking to Parzival later in the text, describes Ither and his relationship to the ladies:

> dich solden hazzen werdiu wîp
> durch sînen minneclîchen lîp:
> sîn dienst was gein in sô ganz,
> ez machte wîbes ougen glanz,
> die in gesâhn, von sîner süeze. (stanza 476: ll. 5–9)

(Because you deprived them of his extremely handsome looks many noble ladies will hate you now; he loved serving them, and his sweet beauty made the eyes of all the ladies who saw him shine.)

He extinguishes both the sight (passive) and the gaze (active) of his comely relative to gratify his own narcissism.

Parzival, oblivious to the gravity of his transgression, continues on his merry way and is hospitably received by the good knight Gurnemanz. After the meal, a bath is prepared for him. Once again, his naked body becomes the object of the gaze of a whole flock of young ladies. This specific passage in the third book of *Parzival* which Lachmann titled "Gastliche Aufnahme" is pivotal to an inquiry into the female gaze. The female ogling described here is an intersection of the sanctioned and non-sanctioned female gaze. It is sexual, but it is recounted in a lighthearted, humorous tone. No negative consequences follow for these anonymous gazing girls, who are never again mentioned.

The scene opens with the narrator's surprise at the sudden appearance of girls, clearly a trope of male fantasy: out of nowhere, pretty girls materialize, ogling and touching the nude male body. Furthermore, the narrator emphasizes that these are not ladies of ill repute, but good girls, "zühte site gelîch." Another indicator that we are dealing with a dream or fantasy is that male nudity, once a common spectacle in classical times, had disappeared completely from the visual landscape of the Middle Ages. Madeline Caviness writes: "by the High Middle Ages, an important cultural shift toward prudery had deprived men as well as women of the sight of the naked athlete . . . nothing could be less naked than a medieval knight in combat, unless his corpse was stripped on the battlefield" (93).

A nude male body was more likely to denote death than scopophilic pleasure. Clearly, that is not the case in the bathing episode. Still, even in a dream sequence, a knight cannot be represented nude and defenseless, exposed to the dangerous gaze of the young women. A fetish is needed to mitigate the threat.

The general purpose of the fetish, within the Freudian system of thought, is to distract from a woman's lack of a penis and her envious gaze when she sees for herself what she does not have. The moment of seeing and knowing is simultaneous, and the male subject needs to alleviate the fear of castration through a fetish.

But what functions as the fetish in the scene of bathing Parzival and the ogling girls? In my view, his nudity is protected under several layers of fetishization. First of all, there is the humorous tone of the scene, the irony of the description that distances and protects Parzival from the castrating gaze of the girls. The girls' clothes, as well, can be read as a fetish; they are objects that cover up, drawing attention away from the "lack" which is the primary purpose of the fetish. Also, the description of the young women's soft white hands might be understood as fetishes or phallic substitutions.[4]

Despite the lighthearted tone, the bathing episode contains a rebuke of female visual curiosity. When the narrator shares his suspicion that the girls would have gladly checked whether the young man had been injured "down below," he disapproves of their behavior (stanza 167: ll. 25–30). In the end, however, the hyperbolic impossibility of the situation mitigates the girls' inappropriateness.

Parzival is further encouraged by his mentor Gurnemanz to remain a pleasing object of the female gaze:

ir müezet dicke wâpen tragen:
so ez von iu kom, daz ir getwagen

under ougen unde an handen sît
(des ist nâch îsers râme zît),
sô wert ir minneclîch gevar:
des nement wîbes ougen war. (stanza 172: ll. 1–6)

(You will wear your armor most of the time. Whenever you take it off, wash the rust off your face and hands; that way, you will look handsome; the ladies' eyes will take note of it.)

Parzival's teacher claims that the main purpose of hygiene is a knight's appeal to ladies. They prefer to look at clean faces. Parzival takes Gurnemanz's advice to heart and rides toward Pelrapeire, where he is seen by a maiden from her window.

sîns rüefens nam dâ niemen war,
wan ein juncvrouwe wol gevar
uz einem venster sach diu magt
den held halden unverzagt. (stanza 182: ll. 15–18)

(Nobody heard his loud shouting except for a young maiden who, from her window, gazed down on the brave hero.)

The text implies that the girl's gaze is not sexual, since there is no reference to the knight's body. Her interest lies in her kingdom, not in Parzival. She assesses his value based on his potential to defend her domain and is ready to send him away if he appears useless in that regard.

An important change occurs in this encounter. Parzival is no longer defined by his beauty; neither the narrator nor the girl even mentions it. Instead of the usual adjective "süeze" he is now described as "helt unverzagt" (stanza 182: l. 18) or as a "werden degen" (stanza 187: l. 2). "Degen," a pars pro toto defining the fighter by his weapon, is a term that was already old-fashioned in Wolfram's time, dating back to the early heroic sagas. Here, its usage further deemphasizes the potentially romantic quality of the encounter, underlining instead the heroic, classical characteristics of the new and improved Parzival.

A little later it becomes clear that the object of the gaze is not Parzival—

even though it is noted that he looks better after the rust is removed—but, instead, the maiden Condwiramurs. I read this development not only as a change in perspective but, since Condwiramurs eventually becomes Parzival's love interest, also as a change in the gendering of Parzival. By taking up the selfless duty of defending Pelrapeire, Parzival undergoes a transformation from object to subject, from pretty girl to valiant knight.

In her book *Feminism and Psychoanalytic Theory*, Nancy Chodorow summarizes the components of the attainment of male gender from a psychoanalytic standpoint:

> First, masculinity becomes and remains a problematic issue for a boy. Second, it involves denial of attachment or relationship, particularly of what the boy takes to be dependence or need for another, and differentiation of himself from another. Third, it involves the repression and devaluation of femininity on both psychological and cultural levels. Finally, identification with his father does not usually develop in the context of a satisfactory affective relationship, but consists in the attempt to internalize and learn components of a not immediately apprehensible role. (34)

Parzival follows the path Chodorow describes as leading to masculine gender identity. He detaches himself from the dependency on his mother, differentiating his plans and goals from those of Herzeloyde. Then, he gradually learns and internalizes the components of his masculine, "knightly" role, obeying the advice of his father figure, Gurnemanz (who is actually his uncle).

The problem is that Parzival's growth is not linear and his gendering within the text is unstable. He relapses into inactivity, into becoming, once again, the inert object of the gaze. While Condwiramurs triggered an appearance of the chivalrous side of his persona, allowing him to become the victorious and selfless defender of Pelrapeire, he regresses into disastrous passivity during his stay in the Grail Castle.

After the fateful meal during which Parzival fails to take the initiative to save the Fisher King, he is pampered and undressed like a helpless baby by handsome pages. Shortly thereafter, naked Parzival is ogled by four young maidens:

vier clâre juncvrouwen
die solten dennoch schouwen
wie man des heldes pflaege
und ob er sanfte laege. (stanza 243: ll. 21–24)

(Four beautiful maidens peeked in; they wanted to see how the knight
was taken care of and whether his bed was soft enough.)

Parzival belatedly jumps under his blanket; the girls already caught an
eyeful of his white-skinned body:

Parzivâl der snelle man
spranc underz declachen.
si sagten: ir sult wachen
durch uns noch eine wîle.
ein spil mit der île
het er unz an den ort gespilt.
daz man gein liehter varwe zilt,
daz begunde ir ougen süezen,
ê si enpfiengen sîn grüezen. (stanza 243: ll. 28–30; stanza 244: ll. 1–6)

(Parzival quickly jumped under his cover. They said to him: Why
don't you stay up with us for a while? Even though he almost won the
little race, he wasn't quite fast enough. Their eyes had already caught
a sweet glimpse of his white body before they received his greeting.)

Knights, of course, routinely posed as objects of the female gaze. In duels,
however, their bodies were completely shielded from view by their suits
of armor. No skin was exposed, and even their faces remained fully invisible. The Grail Castle episode shows us an uncovered, unshielded Parzival,
stripped to the skin, feminized—or, at least, ambiguously gendered as a
white body with red lips. The whiteness of his skin and his nudity bear the
strong imprint of female gendering. One recalls Enite and her swan-white
skin shining through her threadbare dress, or the lightly dressed, unarmed
Erec, who was "blôz als ein wîp" (exposed like a woman). To add further to
the ambiguity, Parzival, a grown man, is completely beardless:

ouch vuogten in gedanke nôt,
daz im sîn munt was sô rôt
unt daz vor jugende niemen dran
kôs gein einer halben gran. (stanza 244: ll. 7–10)

(They were secretly enchanted with his red mouth and his youthful
lack of even half a beard hair.)

The beard is one of the few sex-specific features of medieval bodies as
James Schultz explains: a beard might have identified Parzival as male, but
since he is beardless there is no irrefutable evidence of his gender ("Bodies"
93). Descriptive nouns like "degen" or "held unverzagt" might apply to Parzival only ironically in the encounter with the maidens—lascivious passivity
replaced the masculinity he had displayed earlier. Even his only utterance in
the encounter is passive and transmitted through indirect speech. His chivalrous persona returns later in a nightmare where he is engaged in heavy
fighting, but in his sleep he is also compared to a woman—his mother, Herzeloyde. All the while, the ogling girls are active, aggressive, and probing.
They own the gaze and, thereby, occupy the scopophilic masculine position.

This passage clearly lacks the humor of the bathing scene. The horrible
deed of omission is done and looms large over the doomed Grail Castle.
We learn that the girls are not in Parzival's room by their own will; they
were ordered to keep him company—a fact that forecloses the playfulness
and flirtatiousness that characterized the bathing episode. Hence, these girls
gaze with impunity because they did not choose to be there and because
Parzival's ambiguous gender diffuses the impropriety of the situation.

But why does Parzival's gender fluctuate; why does he oscillate between
the feminine and the masculine, the passive and the active principles? Kathleen Coyne Kelly proposes an intriguing explanation by examining the gaze
dynamics in Arthurian tales. She makes the point that it is only recently
that scholarship has started looking at the representation of the male body,
which had formerly been impervious to the gaze. Although she focuses on
Malory, her thoughts are applicable to German Arthurian material as well.
She writes: "Gaze Theory shows us how, at the precise moment that we expect the male body to be most visible . . . that body is transformed and
feminized, thus shielding the masculine 'body chivalric'" (52).

Parzival's sudden regendering can be read as a way of shielding his male body from the gaze; in particular, the female probing, castrating gaze. If his gender is transformed from masculine to feminine, from active to passive, the nude male form slips unseen through the cracks of the text; it remains intact because it disappeared from sight, leaving behind the already castrated female version of his persona.

In philological scholarship, the regression or failure of a young knight who had previously appeared to be on the right track is traditionally explained with the concept of the *Doppelwegstruktur* (see Dinzelbacher). Iwein and Erec, for example, also suffer a fall from grace. At the end of the narrative they emerge new and improved, fit for all kinds of responsibilities and challenges. The *Iwein* text contains evidence of a regendering/change similar to what we observe in *Parzival*. Parzival's gender slides back and forth along Laqueur's continuum. He remains the object of both the male and the female gaze, whether as an active combatant or as a passive bathing or sleeping beauty. All eyes are off Parzival, however, when another spectacular "gender-confused" creature crashes a feast at the Arthurian court.

Cundrie might be called the Anti-Parzival. He is white-skinned, she is swarthy. He is lovely, she is repulsive. He lacks verbal skills, she knows foreign languages. The text brilliantly juxtaposes the ugly sorceress and the pretty boy who remains mute during her tirade. The narrator criticizes Cundrie for dressing unladylike: "si was niht vrouwenlîch gevar" (stanza 312: l. 15). He paints a rather animalistic picture of her, likening her to a mule, a pig, a dog, a boar, a bear, a monkey, and a lion (stanzas 313, 314). If she hadn't been called a "juncfrouwe" and referred to as "si" we would not have known that this character was female. Even her horse is hideous.

Kundrie bears some resemblance to the Gorgons from ancient Greek myth. In *Medusa*, Stephen Wilk describes their appearance as having scaly heads, tusks, and brazen hands and wings. They had protruding tongues, glaring eyes, and serpents wrapped around their waists as belts. Wilk argues that the disgust, fear, and utter horror caused by Medusa originated in the fear of death and the dead body. He examines photos of putrefied corpses, compares forensic details about freshly deceased people to literary descriptions of Gorgons, and concludes that they are one and the same. Kundrie's repulsiveness, like that of the Gorgons, carries the symbolic message that beauty is ephemeral and skin-deep.

Kundrie is the first person, with the possible exception of Key, who is not impressed with Parzival's external beauty. Her gaze probed him and found him unworthy: "gunêrt sî iuwer liehter schîn / und iuwer manlîchen lide" (stanza 315: ll. 20–21; Shame on your brilliant beauty and your manly strength). She makes the surprising statement: "ich dunke iuch ungehiure, / und bin gehiurer doch dann ir" (stanza 315: ll. 24, 25; You think I am repulsive, but I am a lot less repulsive than you). Cundrie announces that things are not always as they appear. A beautiful boy, for example, might be profoundly ugly on the inside. What seems like trite, conventional wisdom to us moderns is a revolutionary notion in the Arthurian realm, where a connection between nobility of lineage, character, and physical attractiveness is held as self-evident truth. Kundrie's damning speech results in Parzival's temporary disappearance from his own story; that is, he is rendered invisible.

After focusing on Gawain, the narrative swings back to the eponymous hero Parzival in the ninth book. His meeting with a family on pilgrimage is remarkable for the gaze dynamics between him and the beautiful daughters of an old knight, "zwuo juncvrouwen, / die man gerne mohte schouwen" (stanza 446: ll. 17–18). Even though Parzival is clearly attracted to the girls' red-hot lips, "ir munde wârn rôt, dicke, heiz" (stanza 449: l. 28), it is the narrator who wants to steal a kiss from them and who communicates his ideas on ladies' domination over men, inspired by courtly love convention:

wîp sint et immer wîp:
werlîches mannes lîp
hânt si schier betwungen:
in ist dicke alsus gelungen. (stanza 450: ll. 5–8)

(Women will be women. They have no trouble subduing even the strongest man. They've been successful at that a good many times.)

Parzival seems to have an unusual mutual gazing relationship with the girls:

die juncvrouwen im sâhen nâch,
gein den ouch im sîn herze jach

daz er si gerne saehe,

wand ir blic in schoene jaehe. (stanza 451: ll. 27–30)

(The maidens followed him with their gaze while he admitted to himself that they pleased his eyes; their sight declared them beautiful.)

The interlinked, intertwined gaze described in this passage is further emphasized through the fact that "blic" can mean both the active act of gazing as well as "Anblick," being the passive object of someone else's sight. (A similar dual, active-passive meaning exists, of course, for the English word "sight.") Hence, Parzival, who throughout the text shifts from object of the gaze to gazing subject, is suddenly both, simultaneously. Oddly, Parzival's temporary oscillating between a subject/object position of the gaze seems to trigger his conversion, his return, or, to be precise, his first true, conscious commitment to a belief in God. Without further explanation, his change of heart follows immediately after the mutual gazing scene (stanza 452). When he returns to Arthur's court, he takes his rightful place among his fellow knights of the Round Table. He is now no longer a passive visual object of the sexual gaze. His arrival at court signifies the successful completion of his education; he assumes his inherited, sacred responsibilities as a knight, serving the public good. From that point on, all female observers gaze at him admiringly and approvingly—he has transcended his existence as an object of the female sexual gaze and is now seen only as an agent of benevolent power. Order in the patriarchal Arthurian realm has been restored.

6

"Lady, you saw it with your own eyes!"

ENITE AND THE PERFECT FEMALE GAZE IN HARTMANN'S *EREC*

In this chapter I explore Hartmann von Aue's *Erec* with a focus on the main female character, Enite, who is both object of the gaze and gazer herself. Since contemporary readers of medieval romance were to be both entertained and instructed, in what way was the example of Enite instructional? Were female aristocratic readers of the tale encouraged to emulate Enite, or was she, like Der Stricker's walled-in woman, an example of how not to behave?

Even though Enite is the main female personage, she does not appear in the opening of *Erec*; instead, the narrative is propelled forward by the uncourtly behavior of a strange knight and his dwarf. Erec, young and unarmed, is leisurely riding along with Queen Guinevere and her ladies. Suddenly, an unknown knight's diminutive and belligerent companion attacks him. The true reason for Erec's humiliation, however, is not the attack itself but the fact that the queen and her ladies became eyewitnesses of the assault.

> und schamte sich nie so sere
> wan daz diese unere
> diu künegin mit ir vrouwen sach
> als im der geiselslac geschach
> mit grozer schame er wider reit
> also klagete er sin leit (*Erec*, ll. 106–11)

(And the worst part of his shame was that the queen and her ladies watched how he was whipped. He rode back, deeply embarrassed, and told about his suffering.)

When the chastised knight returns to his riding company, he admits that he would have tried to deny the altercation, if only the queen had not seen it with her own eyes:

frouwe ich enmac des niht verlougen
wan irz selbe habet gesehen (ll. 113–14)

(My lady, I can't deny it because you yourself saw it.)

Queen Guinevere, unfortunately for Erec, observed the entire debacle.[1] As a matter of fact, the queen's curious gaze placed Erec in the confrontational situation in the first place. The entire riding party notices the strangers, but it is the queen who insists on knowing more about them. Chrétien de Troyes's version, on which the German text is based, reads as follows: "Queen Guinevere saw the handsome and elegant knight, and she wanted to know who they were" (*Arthurian Romances* 39). The female gaze actively inaugurates the adventure. Since the ladies were watching, Erec could neither ignore nor deny the incident.

It is obvious that Erec is not a battle-tested knight. Unarmed and pretty, he is virtually indistinguishable from his female riding companions. Chrétien's version of *Erec and Enide* emphasizes Erec's immaturity, introducing him as a beautiful body dressed in nice clothes:

Of his great virtues, what to say?
His destrier he rode that day,
sported an ermine cloak, and rode,
galloping, tearing up the road
in front of him. The drapery
of his silk tunic, you could see,
was Constantinople cloth, all fine
flowers of arabesque design.
Stockings he had, superbly cut,

of silk; his spurs were gold; he sat
firm in his stirrups. Accoutrements
of knightly honor and defense
—except his sword—he had not brought. (ll. 97–109)

The narrator mocks the unarmed youth whose excellence is defined by his nice coat and his silk stockings.[2] Erec, like one of the girls, is a passive and defenseless object of the gaze.

After he rides off and arrives at the house of his host, Enite's father, it is Erec's turn to gawk. He intensely ogles her, staring through her threadbare dress at her swan-white skin. The reader sees her through Erec's enamored gaze:

der megede lîp war lobelich.
der roc was grüener varwe,
gezerret begarwe,
abehaere über al.
dar under was ir hemde sal
und ouch zebrochen eteswâ:
sô schein diu lîch dâ
durch wîz alsam ein swan. (ll. 323–30)

(The body of the maiden was praiseworthy. Her dress was green, completely torn and threadbare everywhere. The shirt she wore under the dress was dirty and through the holes in the fabric her white skin shone through, white as a swan.)

The text turns the reader into a voyeur; just like young Erec we peep through her tattered dress, catching a glimpse of her white flesh. The narrator, in his praise of female beauty, provides a generic catalogue, starting with a hyperbolic superlative:

man saget daz nie kint gewan
einen lîp sô gar dem wunsche gelîch:
und waere si gewesen rîch,
sô engebraeste niht ir lîbe
ze lobelîchem wîbe.
ir lîp schein durch ir salwe wât

alsam diu lilje, dâ si stât
under swarzen dornen wîz.
ich waene got sînen vlîz
an si hâte geleit
von schoene und von saelekeit. (ll. 331–41)

(It is said that no other young girl ever compared to her in loveliness. If she had been rich, she would have lacked nothing and she would have been the perfect catch. Her skin gleamed through the shabby clothes like a white lily blooming among thorns. It seems to me that God made a tremendous effort when he created her beauty and grace.)

Medievalists have at times referred to young Enite's enticing, almost dangerous physical appeal and her status as a seductive object of male desire. Joachim Bumke, for example, writes: "Enite [wird]als eine Frau von wunderbarer Schönheit beschrieben, deren Anblick die Welt in Staunen versetzt. . . . Der Anblick ihrer betörenden Schönheit weckt in den Männern eine Liebe, die sich als blinde Begierde äussert und sie alle Rücksichten vergessen lässt" (*Geschichte* 154; Enite is described as a woman of amazing beauty whose sight astounds the world. . . . The sight of her dazzling beauty causes men to love her with blind desire and to act recklessly).

Bumke projects his own preconceived notions of courtly conventions onto Enite; there is nothing in her vague and generic portrait distinguishing her as an object of desire. Actually, the very lack of specificity in the description of female attractiveness is a trope of medieval courtly literature. The beautiful lady lacks concrete features and is adored not as an individual but as an abstract ideal; all the poets exalting feminine beauty appear to be enamored with the identical white-skinned, red-lipped figure. The feminine object of the gaze is distanced, put on a pedestal from where she can barely be seen. Taking a Lacanian viewpoint, she symbolizes uncanny, traumatic otherness and functions as a mirror onto which the male gazer projects his narcissistic ideal; she must remain an inaccessible object or she loses her mystique. Her purpose is to fill the gazer's dream. Lacan describes the idealization of the lady as the elevation of an object into the dignity of "la Chose." The actual object is empty; the woman does not exist.[3]

Erec also projects his ideal of perfect beauty onto Enite, whose body is shrouded in shabby clothes. He shamelessly ogles her from up close, but she does not stare back. She looks down, shyly, modestly, busily occupied with her humble stable-boy duties. She does not talk to him, either. She does not interact at all; in short, Enite is in complete compliance with the behavioral rules taught in courtly didactic literature. When Erec spontaneously asks her father for her hand in marriage, she registers no emotion. Not even her father's insulting commentary that the marriage proposal was probably just a joke elicits a reaction from her.

The host's respectful submission to Erec seems odd; why would he put his trust in someone who unexpectedly materializes on his estate, sans armor, weapons, squires, or any other kind of verification of his nobility? On top of that, Erec is filthy from the long ride and disfigured by the welts the dwarf inflicted on him: "daz ich bin sus zebrochen / under mînen ougen" (ll. 1039–40). And yet, Enite's father is more than willing to simply hand her over to this stranger. Like Parzival, Erec's body apparently bears the indelible mark of his innate and God-given identity as a member of the medieval ruling class. In other words, the look of his body provides sufficient proof of his noble identity; no further authentication is required.

Enite remains silent through further humiliations, such as when Erec refuses to accept her uncle's gift of suitable clothes (ll. 645–49), blatantly disrespecting his wife's public persona and her place in courtly society.[4] She displays a curious deference to her new husband. Even when Ider, the arrogant aggressor, insults her, she does not react (l. 694). She finally shows some emotion, weeping when she believes Erec to be killed during the fight with Ider. Her gaze, much like that of the queen during the dwarf attack, has an effect on Erec, on his willpower and dogged determination to prevail over a more experienced man-at-arms. Erec orders Ider, his lady, and his dwarf to appear before Arthur's court. Interestingly, he does not send them to the king but to the queen; only the lady's gaze could verify his victory (ll. 1080–82).

Enite's, Guinevere's and the anonymous ladies' observation of chivalrous exploits are not mere pastimes—their gaze is essential in a world where knights act and women validate their deeds with their approving, adoring gaze. The female gaze functions as a mechanism of inclusion in this patriarchal system; ladies play the vital role of spectator. The difference between the approving maternal gaze and the critical or sexually desiring gazes stands in for the age-old dichotomy between "woman-as-mother" and "woman-as-whore." The ideal woman-mother gazes in a nonjudgmental way. Like the fairy-tale queen looking in the mirror, the infant receives a message from the mother's gaze, and it is: You are the fairest of them all. An infant's blossoming narcissism is mirrored and sustained by the adoring eyes of the mother. The pure, saintly maiden from the legend of *Der arme Heinrich* lovingly gazes at her master, hideously afflicted with a flesh-eating disease, and sees perfection. Even though she is only a child, her female gaze perceiving the ghastly Lord Heinrich is motherly and nurturing.

The nonmaternal female gaze, however, represents a critical agency, revealing the truth that the man being looked at is perhaps not "vil reine." This other gaze is not idealizing or divinely loving; to the male object of this gaze, it does not reflect back the desired idealized image, and that is a severe transgression against the female gazer's role within the patriarchal scopic economy.[5]

Enite's awakening occurs after her extended honeymoon, while she is in bed with her husband. After mulling over the curses and negative opinions she overhears in the courtyard, she decides to share her concerns with her husband, even though she initially hesitates to do so. This occasion has Enite utter her first recorded words in the lines 3029–32:

si sprach: wê dir, dû vil armer man,
und mir ellendem wîbe,
daz ich mînem lîbe
sô manegen vluoch vernemen sol.

(She spoke: Woe is you, you poor man, and woe is me, poor lowly woman, that I have to hear so many curses.)

King Erec, the celebrated knight, suddenly finds himself at the receiving end of his wife's pity. She finally breaks her silence because, at this juncture, she considers her interference vital; she must save both his life and her own honor. The narrator's assurances regarding Enite's impeccable character, "biderbe unde guot," are tongue-in-cheek; her primary interest lies in keeping up appearances. After all, the grumblings of the court mostly target Enite. "Woe is me!" she laments. Her husband's good name is but an afterthought—a clear infraction of how a proper wife should conduct herself.

Both Enite and Erec have made mistakes, and both will have to undergo a process of purification through a drawn-out learning experience. Enite's lack of discretion and reticence propels the action forward; she uncovers and reveals elements of the secret world of men, and she will pay dearly for this transgression.

In her article "Enide's Disruptive Mouths," E. Jane Burns analyzes the figure of Enide, Enite's French counterpart in Chrétien de Troyes's version of the adventure. Burns argues that female bodies in male-authored medieval literature are not as easily colonized as female speech. Burns theorizes the existence of a subnarrative running through and counter to the patriarchal main narrative, told by the bodies of fictional maidens. Female bodies, female voices, female gazes—all are represented in the frequently misogynous fantasies of male authors, but they can also be isolated and used to rewrite the stories in which they appear. Burns embraces a sociocultural reading, showing "how the lady's portrait embodies not women as subjects but medieval culture's ambivalent fear of and desire for women" (*Bodytalk* 13). So, even if female figures in male-authored romance only contain traces of real medieval women, I agree with Burns that we do learn about medieval women from these patriarchal texts; a trace, after all, is better than nothing at all.

After hearing Enite's unwelcome news update regarding his court, Erec decides that it is time for a road trip. He commands his bride to get ready by putting on her prettiest dress:

> zehant hiez er si ûf stân,
> daz si sich wol kleite
> unde ane leite
> daz beste gewaete
> daz si iender haete. (ll. 3053–57)

(He immediately told her to get up and get dressed, to put on the best clothes that she owned.)

By ordering Enite to dress in her finest clothes, Erec reverses his stance on the irrelevance of a woman's apparel compared to the beauty of her body. He had forced her to appear at Arthur's court in rags when they were first married:

man sol einem wîbe
kiesen bî dem lîbe
ob si ze lobe stât
unde niht bî der wât. (ll. 646–49)

(For a woman, it is her body that should determine whether she is praiseworthy, not her clothing.)

The obvious explanation for this incongruous change of heart is that, at the royal court, Erec wanted to brag through understatement: My queen is prettier than all the other ladies combined, even wearing nothing but rags. However, for this upcoming adventure, planned for the sole purpose of restoring his honor, he won't take any chances. He wants Enite to attract other men with both physical beauty and expensive clothes. Erec sends his wife ahead of him as a decoy, an attractive object of the gaze and desire of strangers whom the two encounter on the long road ahead. Obviously, Erec is aware of the danger to which he exposes Enite. He even doubles down on the risk by demanding her silence, knowing she would want to alert him of impending attacks. He puts her in the position of a lookout, without allowing her to communicate what she sees.

Riding through a forest under the light of the moon, the couple is spotted by three lurking brigands. Enide sees them first since she is riding ahead (ll. 3123–24). She quickly assesses the situation and identifies the men as robbers:

diz was ir êrstez herzeleit
daz ir zuo der verte geschach
wan si an ir gebaerden sach
daz si roubaere wâren (ll. 3125–28)

(This was the first time on the trip that she had to endure heartache; she saw from their body language that they were robbers.)

The text contains a humorous description of how Enite tries to communicate with Erec without speaking:

si wolde imz mit gebâren
gerne kunt hân getân.
dô enmohte ers niht verstân (ll. 3129–31)

(She tried her best to communicate it to him through body language,
but he simply couldn't understand her.)

The reader is called to imagine the wild gesticulation, pointing, miming,
and grimacing. Incidentally, the fact that her husband cannot decode Enite's
paralinguistic signals indicates a problem within their relationship, which
up to this point was based solely on sexual attraction. There clearly is a failure to communicate. Enite eventually grows frustrated with her husband's
inability or refusal to get the message.

After a long inner monologue, she makes the painful decision to speak,
regardless of his "Verbot": "sich ûf, lieber herre" (l. 3182; Just look up, my
dear lord). Not only does she disobey him, she actually commands him
to do something. Her words mirror the situation that got her into trouble
in the first place. Again, she calls on him to open his eyes. In the episode
at court she also saw something that had escaped him, verbally commu-
nicating her superior vision to him. No matter how excessively polite her
comment is phrased—"ûf genâde verre / wil ich dir durch triuwe sagen" (ll.
3183–84)—the fact remains that her unrepressed urge to speak represents
a twofold problem: first, it is an infraction of his direct, lordly order to remain silent; and second, it is a revelation that—much to his shame—she sees
things that he does not. Her field of vision is larger than his, and her critical
gaze penetrates where his does not. Enite's role is that of a prophet, in the
original sense of the word: she is a seer.[6]

Enite's first infraction, her disobedience, is a trope of medieval literature:
the evil wife, or "übel wîp." The theme reoccurs in innumerable popular
tales circulating mostly in non-noble (ignoble?) layers of medieval society. For example, the misogynous tale of the "übel Adelheit" enjoyed great
popularity. This story is about a townsman who is unhappily married to
a bully and who uses reverse psychology on her to get what he wants. He
decides to trick his wife into plunging to her death by warning her not to

walk so close to the river. Of course, she disobeys, falls, and drowns. Her liberated husband remarks in good humor that her corpse must surely be drifting upstream, considering how contrary she was in life (Weddige, *Mittelhochdeutsch* 148–53).

The negative stereotypes against women contained in the tale of Adelheit are mirrored in Erec's reaction to Enite's speech. He seems to be saying "typical!" He knows all about women's nature, and Enite's disobedience fits the profile:

daz ich von wîben hân vernomen,
daz ist wâr, des bin ich komen
vol an ein ende hie:
swaz man in unz her noch ie
alsô tiure verbôt,
dar nâch wart in alsô nôt
daz sis muosten bekorn.
ez ist doch vil gar verlorn
swaz man iuch mîden heizet,
wan daz ez iuch reizet
daz irz enmuget vermîden:
des sult ir laster lîden.
swaz ein wîp nimmer getaete,
der irz nimmer verboten haete,
niht langer si daz verbirt
wan unz ez ir verboten wirt:
sô enmac sis langer niht verlân. (ll. 3242–58)

(What I had heard about women, I now find confirmed. Whatever they are told to avoid tempts them so much that they can't help themselves. It is completely useless to forbid you to do something; the temptation will overcome you and you won't resist it: for that, you will be punished. Something a woman would never do if she were allowed to do it she will do immediately once it is forbidden. She simply can't help herself.)

We encountered the age-old assumption that women will inevitably overstep boundaries in the biblical account of Eve gazing at the forbidden fruit and desiring it. Even though she has permission to pick any other fruit in paradise, she chooses the one she is not allowed to have. This same line of reasoning is also found in the *huote* discursus of Gottfried von Strassburg's *Tristan*; the text warns that women always want what is forbidden and, consequences be damned, they will take it anyway.

Enite apologizes for her disobedience and promises never again to speak without permission: "Ez geschiht mir nimmer mêre" (l. 3265; It won't happen again). However, shortly after this incident she finds herself in a situation quite similar to the first one. The couple once again encounters thieves; this time there are five, not three. Enite personifies an irresistible prize, which means that Erec's plan worked—Enite functions well as robber bait. In an attempt to warn him silently, Enite turns around on her horse to give Erec an alarmed look. According to Thomasin von Zerclaere's *Der Welsche Gast*, a text we examined in chapter 1, the action of looking around while riding is an infraction of good manners. So, even though she is not speaking, she is still misbehaving. To make matters worse, Enite disobeys yet another one of the rules of conduct for noble ladies: she talks too much.

Oddly, Thomasin's treaty on proper behavior, written after Hartmann composed *Erec*, holds up Enite, guilty of at least the two above-mentioned faux pas, as an example to his young readers. I can think of only one explanation for Thomasin's choice of Enite as a role model: he implicitly recommends an emulation of the early, pre-marriage Enite, or the later, silenced, submissive Enite.

Enite's transformation from a young wife who is alert to her surroundings into a passive, saint-like figure begins when her husband confronts the brutal count Oringles. After defeating and mortally wounding Erec, the count abducts Enite. At his castle, Oringles unlawfully tries to claim her as his wife, justifying his violence against her with a graceless echo of the anonymous love poem "Frauenlied": "Du bist mîn, ich bin dîn" (see Moser and Tervooren 21):

> Si ist mîn und bin ich ir:
> wie welt ir daz erwern mir,
> ich entuo ir swaz mir gevalle? (ll. 6546–48)

(She is mine and I am hers, how could you hold me back from doing to her whatever I want?)

She resolutely resists his advances, preferring death to a life with the count:

und swaz mir von iu geschiht,
unde nemet ir mir den lîp,
ich enwirde doch nimmer iuwer wîp.
des nemet iu ein zil. (ll. 6573–76).

(Whatever might happen to me by your hand, even if you killed me, I will never be your wife. Keep that in mind.)

A young woman refusing a marriage because she wants to be free to serve her Lord, even under the threat of being killed, is a trope of medieval hagiographical accounts. The vita of Saint Agnes, for example, tells the story of this maiden-saint who was martyred in the third century for her refusal to marry the son of a powerful man (see Cazelles, *Lady as Saint*). Incidentally, the vita contains a harsh condemnation of the voyeuristic gaze: onlookers anticipating Agnes's death at the stake go up in flames themselves, while the girl is initially spared.

Enite, as well, becomes a saintly figure and transforms from an active gazer into a passive object of the gaze, like Saint Agnes on the stake. Unlike the saint, though, Enite does not refuse marriage; since she is a courtly character, her devotion is not to God but to her knight. Enite thus represents a link between the sacred and the profane: she symbolizes the connection between Mariolatry and courtly love, which, in the Freudian paradigm, have a common origin in the male psyche.

After Erec's miraculous resurrection and subsequent berserker-like rampage, the guests of the failed wedding disperse, horrified at the ungodly apparition and threat posed by the angry, sword-wielding knight. Only Enite retains her Zen-like calm in the midst of pandemonium. Her eyes delight in the vision of her husband:

sîn getorste dâ niemen bîten
âne vrouwen Eniten.

den tôten si vil gerne sach:
ze liebe wart ir ungemach (ll. 6682–85)

(Nobody dared to wait for him, besides for Lady Enite. She was thrilled
to see the dead man walking, and her sadness turned to joyous love.)

Once the happily reunited couple is back on the road, they have to share
a horse; Enite sits in front, Erec in back. Even though her location on the
horse should allow for a better view, she cannot see any further ahead than
he. The distance between the two has shrunk, literally and figuratively, but
Enite paid dearly for the realignment of their relationship: she lost her edge
and her ability to foresee events. When she tells him of the occurrences he
missed during his period of unconsciousness, she enlightens him with her
insight and her perceptive mind for the last time. The end of her narration
marks the completion of her transformation. It is significant that her eyes
hurt and that she cries at the end:

nû tete si im die sache
ir ougen zungemache
allez weinende kunt. (ll. 6768–70)

(Under tears, and with her eyes hurting, she told him all that had
happened.)

Her cathartic tears coincide with her complete and utter surrender to
Erec and the female condition. The religious tone of the conversion is unmistakable. Tears as a sign of female rehabilitation also appear in other medieval texts. In *Parzival*, Jeschute sheds tears after her unfortunate encounter with Parzival. Her husband, the proud Orilus, predicts: "ich sol velwen
iuweren rôten munt, / [und] iuwern ougen machen roete kunt" (stanza 136:
ll. 5, 6; Your lips will lose their color and your eyes will turn red).

Enite's obligatory tears also remind us of those shed by Griselda, the classic medieval example of a paragon of virtue. Griselda never questions her
husband's judgment, even when his actions reach incomprehensible lev-
els of cruelty and arbitrary injustice. Even though Griselda is not a saint,
she is still a martyr, a "maternal martyr" (see B. Newman, *Virile Woman*).
Griselda's story, much like Enite's, culminates in the shedding of tears. A
similarly lachrymose climax is found in the Griselda-esque medieval tale of

"König Drosselbart" (*Grimms Märchen*). Here, a proud princess mocks the physical appearance of a suitor. Her father, the king, dislikes the attitude of his daughter and gives her in marriage to the first beggar that comes to the castle gate. All the way to her new husband's cottage she laments: "Ach, ich arme Jungfer zart! Hätt' ich genommen den König Drosselbart!" (Woe is me, poor delicate virgin. If only I had taken King Drosselbart in marriage!). She eventually learns the value of hard work as a kitchen hand at the king's wedding. Trying to sneak a peek at the festivities, she realizes that the beggar and the king are one and the same person. She had gazed with desire at her own wedding celebration. In the end she tearfully apologizes for her prideful behavior and the couple lives happily ever after, or so the story goes.

Tears clean medieval women's eyes from the impurities of critical judgment. *Der Renner*, a text discussed in chapter 2, also contains numerous emphatic admonitions that women should not judge men on visual appeal but should somehow focus on what lies beneath the surface. "Physical beauty is only skin-deep" is the message, and girls' superficiality is the reason for the failure to see inner values. A woman who gazes at a man should do so in an uncritical and motherly fashion; she should be ever mindful of his pride and his important role in society. Her own role is to support and to adore him.

The reformed version of Enite has now completely lost her ability to foresee danger. When Erec inadvertently fights his old friend, the dwarf Guivreiz, Enite remains uninvolved. Erec, for his part, did not see anything, either, but he did hear Guivreiz and his entourage approaching:

dô si noch wâren verre,
der ellende herre
wart vil wol gewar
der gewâfenten schar,
wan der schal und der dôz
was von den schilten grôz. (ll. 6872–77)

(When they were still far apart from each other, the noble stranger became aware of the heavily armed group approaching, because of the great noise that they made with their shields.)

Enite sees Erec's weakness, "wan si sîn unkraft gesach" (l. 6891), but either she learned her lesson to keep her mouth shut or she simply no longer feels the urge to speak up. She is above it all; this is a side effect of her new saintly perfection.

Enite soon has another reason for letting her tears flow. Erec, in an attempt to wholly restore his reputation, accepts the challenge of the Joie de la Curt, the toughest of all fights.

> nû enwart vrouwen Enîten
> sorge nie mê sô groz:
> der regen ir von den ougen vlôz (ll. 8657–59)

> (This was the greatest sorrow Enite ever had in her life; tears fell like rain from her eyes.)

Her crying seems well justified: Erec's chances of survival appear slim at best. Mabonagrin, his opponent, has killed every single challenger for the past twelve years. (Talk about a winning streak!) Erec's high-stakes duel presents itself as an all-or-nothing deal. He will either win the tremendous honor of having vanquished the magnificent Mabonagrin, or die trying.

The old Enite's keen perception, openness, and awareness of her surroundings are no longer present in the newly improved Enite. Like the "Dreiweisheitsaffen," the three wise monkeys who symbolize wisdom, she neither sees nor hears nor speaks. She does not warn her husband, she does not lament or pronounce her objections. All she can do is let her tears flow. The formerly energetic heroine now resembles the eighty bloodless, lifeless damsels who do nothing but cry all day long:

> daz bluot ir hiufeln entweich:
> dô wurden nase und wengel bleich.
> daz machete in der ougen regen (ll. 8318–20)

> (All blood completely drained out of their noses and cheeks and they became white; this was because of the tears raining from their eyes.)

These ladies spend their lives waiting for a knight to finally free them. Enite, like a chameleon, becomes indistinguishable from the damsels; it is almost as if her color now exactly matches the pale skin tone of these unfortunate creatures. Actually, at the beginning of the story, Enite was already swan-white and silent, so she is just reverting to her original state. She suffers a crying spell after which her eyes and ears give out along with her knees; she faints and collapses:

> diu kraft ir zuo der varwe entweich,
> und wart tôtvar und bleich
> und viel vor leide in unmaht.
> der liehte tac wart ir ein naht,
> wan si gehôrte noch gesach. (ll. 8824–28)

(Strength and color drained out of her and she became white as a corpse; her suffering made her lose consciousness. Day turned to night for her and she lost the ability to hear or see.)

Just like the damsels, Enite does not witness the duel. Hence, she does not even fulfill one of the more traditional roles of the Arthurian heroine: gazing at and cheering for her fighting knight. Enide, Enite's French counterpart, does not watch the fight, either. In Dorothy Gilbert's verse translation of *Erec et Enide* we read:

> He kissed her, and to God's mercy
> commended her. So, too, did she,
> for him; still in anxiety,
> because she could not ride and go,
> follow, see for herself, and know
> this outcome, how he'd expedite
> whatever task this was, or fight.
> So she remained, to wait, to grieve,
> since there was no alternative;
> sad, fearful of the aftermath. (Chrétien de Troyes, *Erec and Enide*, ll.
>   5848–57)

Both in Chrétien's and in Hartmann's version, Enide/Enite has a new role: passively waiting and crying. No more chivalrous adventures for this young lady! Her spirit and her lively personality have simply evaporated. What a sad, anticlimactic ending to such a promising female character who, on several occasions, heroically and cleverly saved the life of her husband.

The way Enite looks at her husband at the end of this Arthurian romance is what renders her happy ending possible. The good lady Enite no longer sees, her eyesight dulled by tears of remorse, despair, and saintly bliss. She now functions as a mirror, reflecting her knight's accomplishments, his worth and his valor. She relinquished her threatening position of superiority to conform to the patriarchal ideal of the perfect female persona: reassuring and supportive rather than critical.

7

Knight or Eye Candy?

THE GENDERING GAZE IN HARTMANN VON AUE'S *IWEIN*

The queen awakes from her nap and walks in on an informal gathering of knights who are listening to Kalogrenant recount an adventure. Even though there is nothing to see, the storyteller "projects" and reenacts the event, turning his audience into spectators. The sleepy queen suddenly finds herself in the traditional role of a noble lady watching knightly pursuit. This time, though, she was not an invited guest; she had inadvertently and inconveniently infiltrated an all-male gathering. Not surprisingly, Kalogrenant hesitates to continue his tale about a confrontation that ended in abject defeat and humiliation. Courtly ladies were supposed to witness only successful quests. Kalogrenant, the failed hero, is fully aware that he left a stain on the glossy image of Arthurian knighthood; another knight must now blot it out.

In this case, it is the young knight Iwein who takes up the challenge and deliberately, without waiting for the king's official blessing, sets out to repair the cracked Round Table. The queen will not see young Iwein's actual quest to restore the good name of his brother-in-arms, but she will surely hear about it later. Also, many other noble ladies witness his adventures. In addition to the ogling female characters, the narrator's extra-diegetic gaze on Iwein stands in for the female gaze. Thus, reading and listening women can "observe" the adventure, albeit with narrative delay.

In the following pages I will look closely at the diegetic gaze of female characters populating Hartmann von Aue's poem *Iwein*. The outside gaze, meaning contemporary readership of romances, was also primarily female.

The countless dedications to their doyenneship at the beginning of manuscripts point to the conclusion that ladies played an active role in the writing of Arthurian romance, even though, with the exception of Marie de France, they did not themselves author any of the poems. *Iwein*, in particular, exemplifies how male medieval poets focused on female audiences, composing specifically for this readership, customizing the narrative to the ladies' approving gaze.

The main female personage in *Iwein* is Lunete, a maiden in the service of Lady Laudine. Lunete secretly watches Iwein during his fight with the lord of the realm which Iwein unlawfully entered. She recognizes him as the only knight who courteously greeted her during a visit to Arthur's court. She reminds him of this fact:

> herre, do gruozetet ir mich,
> und ouch dâ nieman mêre.
> do erbutet ir mir die êre
> der ich iu hie lônen sol.
> herre, ich erkenn iuch wol (ll. 1194–98)

(Sir, you and you alone greeted me back then. You honored me in that way then for which I will repay you now. Yes, lord, I recognize you well.)

One might read this passage as a critique of male courtly behavior. Only a single knight actually lived up to the ideals of chivalry? All the others rudely ignored both the girl and the rules of conduct? It turns out that Iwein acted not only courteously but shrewdly when he greeted Lunete at Arthur's court; his small gesture paid off handsomely when she supplies him with some rather useful magical objects.[1]

Lunete rewards Iwein with a magic ring which renders the wearer invisible—a handy device, especially when one is pursued by heavily armed guards. As an added bonus, the ring keeps Iwein hidden from the grief-stricken lady he turned into a widow.

It is surprising how often valiant knights, with no apparent damage to their reputation or status, are saved by women. Eneas (discussed in chapter 4) enjoys the generosity and hospitality of Queen Dido; after her demise he quickly gets on with his life. Erec, the young king (whom we encountered in chapter 6), escaped death at least three times thanks to the foresight and negotiating skills of his wife, Enite.

Iwein also breathes easy under the protection of a woman. But not for long. The vision of Lady Laudine, the beguiling widow, takes his breath away. In a humorous reversal of a medieval trope, the invisible Iwein longingly ogles the beautiful lady from a window:

> wande sî nâch sîner bete
> ein venster ob im ûf tete,
> und liez si in wol beschouwen (ll. 1449–52)

(Then she opened a window because he asked for it; that way he could have a good look at her.)

Solidly camouflaged, "sam daz holz under der rinden" (l. 1208; like wood under the bark), a passive Iwein looks down at the widow, from the cozy shelter of a "kemenaten," a distinctively feminine space. He ogles her naked skin shimmering through the dress which she tore in an expression of grief. Her lament is skillfully and deliberately constructed, in spite of her emotional turmoil. She taunts and teases in an attempt to trick the hidden murderer of her husband into revealing himself:

> wie mac er dar an verzagen
> ern lâze sich ouch ein wîp sehen?
> wand wuz möht im von der geschehen? (ll. 1400–1402)

(How could he possibly be scared to show himself to a woman? What could she possibly do to him?)

Why wouldn't he come out? What could possibly happen to him if a poor little woman saw him? she is asking, loud enough for him to hear every word. He doesn't bite and stays put; he knows full well that if he emerged now, the guards would quickly apprehend and kill him.

Laudine's grief performance is prompted by her acute awareness of being a spectacle, of being watched not only by her court, which is scrutinizing her behavior for an appropriate showing of grief, but also by the killer. She is absolutely convinced that he is still near; she even has what passes for scientific proof: the wounds of her slain husband reopen in the presence of the murderer:

> Nû ist uns ein dinc geseit
> vil dicke vür die wârheit,
> swer den andern habe erslagen,
> und wurder vür in getragen,
> swie langer dâ vor waere wunt,
> er begunde bluoten anderstunt. (ll. 1355–60)

(Now we have been assured that one thing is certain; if someone has killed a man and that man is being brought near his killer, the wound bleeds anew, no matter how long ago it was inflicted.)

The death of her husband threw Laudine's kingdom into grave peril; without male protection her hold on the domain is tenuous. Laudine's loud declarations and her public performance of grief, therefore, have a political objective; she needs the sympathy, support, and loyalty of her court. Whether she personally regrets her bellicose husband's demise is unknowable and irrelevant.

Laudine's elaborate public production of mourning and the spectacle she becomes presuppose her knowledge of being the object of the gaze. Her elegant speech suggests a spontaneous cry from the heart, but the rhetorical refinement indicates a calculated theatrical performance designed for a specific audience:

> waz sol ich unsaelic wîp?
> ouwê daz ich ie wart geborn!
> ouwê wie hân ich dich verlorn?
> ouwê, trutgeselle! (ll. 1468–71)

(What shall become of me, unlucky woman? Why, oh why was I ever born! Why, oh why did I have to lose you? Why, oh why, beloved!)

After a lament in which she portrays herself as a helpless woman, she continues on for three verses, all starting with "ouwê," the third of which is dramatically missing two legs, cut short, like the life of her murdered husband.

All the while, Iwein breathlessly watches the mesmerizing show from his hideaway, concealed by Lunete and her magic ring. The window from which he observes Laudine becomes a framing device, turning the female shape into a two-dimensional moving image for visual consumption. Iwein stares at Laudine; he is so passive, so immobile that he did not even open the window by himself. Lunete had to do it for him. Iwein is utterly smitten with the unscrolling visual feast. He perceives the window itself as the source of his thrill.

> Her Iwein saz verborgen
> in vreuden unde in sorgen.
> im schuof daz venster guot gemach,
> des er genôz daz er sî sach (ll. 1691–94)

> (Lord Iwein sat, hidden, in joy and in sorrow. The window made him happy because it allowed him to see her.)

The window acquires the function of an eye or a camera; it is Iwein's only connection to the outer world. He himself is literally invisible and does not take part in the life around him; just as the eye is a person's most important sensual organ in connecting to the outside world, Iwein's window negates his invisibility and bridges his isolation by allowing him to take part through observation.

The visual object Iwein enjoys while secretly peering out the window is the perfect form of a woman. He also perceives her suffering and her physical expressions of grief, both of which inconveniently affect his gratification. He does not empathize with her as a suffering human being but, instead, expresses approval of her beauty and annoyance at her grief.

> Ouwê waz hât ir getân
> ir antlütze unde ir schoeniu lîch,
> der ich nie niht sach gelîch?
> ichn weiz waz sî zewâre
> an ir goltvarwem hâre
> und an ir selber richet,
> daz sî den lîp zebrichet.
> dâ ist sî selbe unschuldec an (ll. 1668–75)

(Oh, no, what did her beautiful face and body that have no equal ever do to her? I don't know why she punishes herself and her golden hair, why she hurts her body when she is clearly innocent.)

Here, Iwein reminds us of another one of Hartmann's characters: the count of Oringles, to whom we were introduced in chapter 6. The count is equally impatient and annoyed with Enite's expression of grief over the loss of her slain husband. This obvious similarity is complicated by the fact that Iwein is repeatedly praised as a good and valiant Arthurian knight, while the count of Oringles is portrayed as a villain. Oringles, just like Iwein, sees the woman before him not as a human being but as a spectacle. Her sorrow remains invisible, hence incomprehensible to him. When Enite tries to end her life out of despair and sadness, he asks her:

> saget, wunderlîchez wîp,
> war umbe woldet ir den lîp
> selbe hân ersterbet
> und an iu hân verderbet
> daz schoeniste bilde
> daz zam oder wilde
> ie mannes ouge gesach? (*Erec*, ll. 6160–66)

(Speak, strange woman, why would you want to kill that beautiful body or spoil the prettiest picture which, tame or wild, was ever seen by man's eye?)

The count of Oringles fails to understand why Enite would want to destroy the beautiful apparition, the "bilde" she represents to him and other men. Isn't being a feast for male eyes reason enough to live? He decides that he wants her to be his wife, since she is the prettiest woman he ever saw:

> daz er bî sînen zîten
> nâhen noch wîten
> nie schoener wîp hete gesehen:
> ouch begunden ims die ritter jehen. (ll. 6180–83)

(In his time he had never seen a prettier woman far or wide; his knights said the same thing.)

Of course, it only encourages him that his followers remark on the unusual beauty of this found woman, thereby elevating Oringles to the object of their admiration and envy should he succeed in his pursuit. A psychoanalytic reading of this passage suggests that his masculinity would be validated by possessing her; the beautiful woman functions as the phallus through which men gain elevated status in the eyes of other men. He desires to have what her beauty brings to his relationship with other men.

Iwein also burns with the desire to possess a woman whom he only knows through ogling her from afar, during her public performance of grief and loss. Surprisingly, Lunete takes his side, using a well-constructed rhetorical argument to browbeat her mistress, Lady Laudine, into a marriage with her husband's murderer—sight unseen. Lunete functions as a patriarchal agent; she enters into an alliance with Iwein using Lady Laudine as an object of exchange, a payment for services rendered.

Laudine ponders her servant's logical argument and arrives at the same conclusion. The knight who vanquished and killed her husband must have been the better man. Hence, he is perfectly well equipped to become guardian of her person and her domain. Laudine's watchful gaze is not enough; she needs the oversight of a male companion.

Curiously, Minne, the love goddess, makes an appearance to seal the deal, prompting Laudine to fall in love with Iwein before she ever lays eyes on him. This twist of events is implausible, a deus ex machina device to explain Laudine's change of heart. After all, the only thing Laudine knows for sure about Iwein is that he provoked and killed her husband. How could such a maneuver inspire affection? The author/narrator takes a lazy shortcut with this improbable arrival of love personified.[2] The nature of Iwein's attraction to Laudine is simpler: he likes what he sees, and it doesn't hurt that the object of his gaze is wealthy and available.

After the wedding and the big hoopla of Arthur's arrival, Gawain convinces Iwein to leave his bride and go on "aventiure" with him. Under the scrutiny of Arthur's court and the chivalric value system, Laudine has no choice but to give her blessings for the journey. She hands Iwein a magic ring as a memento. The sparkly jewel is a stand-in for her own beauty, and its presence on Iwein's hand is to remind him of Laudine's ultimatum of returning within one year.

unde lât diz fingerlin
einen geziuc der rede sîn.
ichn wart nie manne sô holt
dem ich diz selbe golt
wolde lîhen ode geben. (ll. 2945–49)

(And let this ring bear witness to our agreement. I have never loved a man so much that I would have wanted to give or lend him this golden ring.)

Laudine fully appreciates the fragility of their relationship, which is based on his visual attraction to her. She fears that he will forget her once he is removed from her physical presence. She tells him that the ring represents her body; she never entrusted the ring to anyone else because she never trusted another man like Iwein. Furthermore, she instructs him in the ring's happiness-bestowing and protective magical powers.

er muoz wol deste baz leben
der ez treit und an siht.
her Iwein, nûne verliesetz niht.
sînes steines kraft ist guot:
er gît gelücke und senften muot:
er ist saelec der in treit. (ll. 2950–55)

(The one who wears this ring and has it before his eyes will live a better life. Do not lose it, Lord Iwein! The power of the stone is extraordinary: it bestows happiness and contentment: whoever wears it is blessed.)

Iwein does wear the magical ring on his adventures, and it protects him from physical harm. It does not, however, fulfill the main purpose for which Laudine gave it to him—as a remembrance of her vision and the deadline for his return. He fails to come back within a year, and the consequences of his forgetfulness are dire. He loses the love, trust, and domain of Laudine and, as a result, descends into mental darkness. When Iwein falls from grace—a movement typical of the Arthurian knight's "Doppelweg"—his total decline coincides with his transformation from active voyeur into the passive object of the female gaze.

When Iwein offends Laudine and loses her love, he also loses his "other." His heroic character existed primarily through the figurative gaze of Laudine as his audience, whether or not she was physically present. She was always there as the "postulated" gazer whenever he performed his knightly feats. He had wanted to avoid Erec's fate, the "verligen" (lazy loafing about, sleeping in, underachieving) which was also evoked by Gawain,[3] but Iwein overshot his goal and lost his knightly raison d'être. His crisis is considerably more serious than the vexing embarrassment experienced by Erec. Iwein's descent into the depths of human existence, his change from subject to object, from man to animal, also mark a switch in gender roles. If the active penetrating gaze is male, as Freud and Mulvey theorize, the loss of the gaze signals a phallic loss. Freud describes the phallic qualities of the gaze in his essay "Das Unheimliche." Being blinded and being castrated are, in dreams and myths, identical. Iwein's eyes are closed, and he is completely naked when he becomes a passive object of the gaze:

> er lief nû nacket beider,
> der sinne unde der cleider,
> unz daz in zeinen stunden
> slâfende vunden
> drî vrouwen dâ er lac,
> wol umb einen mitten tac (ll. 3359–64)

> (He was completely stripped of both his mind and his clothes when, one day, three ladies found him sleeping along the road, in the middle of the day.)

Apparently, Iwein has lost not only his ability to talk but also his sense of decency and shame. He is naked, unarmed, and unaware of his environment, the exact opposite of what a knight should be. Iwein falls asleep near a road, in bright daylight. He is napping in plain sight of a group of courtly ladies who happen to ride by:

> nâ ze guoter mâze
> bî der lantstrâze
> diu in ze rîten geschach (ll. 3365–67)

(rather near a country road along which they happened to ride at the time)

The ladies choose not to avert their eyes, but instead stare at Iwein's exposed body with great interest. One of them closely leans in to take a better look:

> und alsô schiere do in ersach
> diu eine vrouwe von den drin,
> dô kêrte sî über in
> und sach in vlîzeclîchen an (ll. 3368–71)

(As soon as one of the three ladies had seen him she leaned over him and gave him a very close look.)

This scene is remarkably humorous. The ironic categorization of the curious young lady as "vlîzeclîch" in her examination of the naked knight not only excuses female eroticized gazing pleasure, scopophilia, or "Schaulust" as Freud called it, but re-labels it as Christian charity. Obviously, a more charitable action would have been to drape something over the exposed male body.

I think that this Arthurian text purposefully plays with the dichotomy that exists in the medieval concept of the female gaze. As I have argued before, the female gaze in medieval texts occurs as a forbidden sexual gaze but also as a supportive, admiring motherly gaze. The former had to be severely suppressed, since it had the potential to destabilize social order, which was based on women's passivity as objects of exchange between men. Women gazing in a direct and erotic way might lead to their choosing of sexual partners, thereby shaking the foundation of the patriarchal kinship system. The supportive female gaze, however, functioned as a pillar of patriarchal society, since an approving, loving female gaze supplied male objects of the gaze with the confidence and confirmation they needed in order to take on societal tasks and responsibilities, not to mention chivalrous pursuits, both in real military challenges and in tournaments. I argue, therefore, that the obligatory female observation of male pursuit differed substantially from the condemned sexual gaze.

Through a humorous treatment of the intricate and delicate subject matter of female gazing, Hartmann's text wriggles out of the possible reproach of subverting patriarchal values. By calling the ladies' conduct a charitable act, he covers up or even erases the scandal of their sexual gazing; as a result, there is no destabilization of social order as perpetrated by Herzeloyde, Dido, or Enite. To be sure, the girls clearly look at a male body in a sexual way, but the text shields them by claiming that it is done in charity and curiosity, not sexual desire.

When the younger lady returns to the naked knight she indulges not only in sexual gazing but also in hands-on exploration of Iwein's body, going far beyond what is necessary for the application of healing ointment. The text emphasizes her eagerness to run her fingers all over his body, from head to toe:

> mit ter vil edelen salben
> bestreich si in allenthalben
> über houbet und über vüeze.
> ir wille was sô süeze
> daz sî daz alsô lange treip
> unz in der bühsen niht beleip. (ll. 3475–80)

(She slathered the precious ointment all over his body. She was so sweetly devoted to his recovery that she continued until she had used up the whole container.)

Again, her visual and manual inspection of his exposed body is humorously cloaked in compassion and in a desire to restore him to health so that he might help her mistress fight off the evil Count Aliers. The text recodes this one-sided sexual encounter as the socially praiseworthy act of a Good Samaritan, and she escapes the narrator's and the contemporary audience's judgment.

Iwein's predicament has additional implications. For one thing, the depiction of male nudity is extremely rare in the Arthurian cycle. Knights normally covered up their whole bodies to the point that they sometimes failed to recognize old friends or relatives on the battlefield, as happened between Erec and Guivreiz, or Parzival and Gawain. Their armor and all their clothes would not come off publicly until they were dead, as in the case of Ither in *Parzival*. I believe that Iwein's nudity cannot be understood as public nudity either, as it is only visible to the three ladies. Even though the text informs us that the girl looks directly at Iwein's naked body, we do not share her vision—his body remains hidden. In a way, through the way the narrative is structured, we only "see" her seeing him. The gazing women are the visual object of the narrator's and readers' gaze. This view fits with Laura Mulvey's conclusion that, no matter what, women are always the object of the gaze. The male body is veiled and only hinted at. There is no top-to-toe catalogue of the naked knight; in fact, the only "body part" specific to Iwein is his scar by which the girl identifies him.

The readers of the romance, however, are not the only ones shielded from Iwein's nudity; the girl takes great pains to also protect Iwein himself from becoming aware of his exposure. After she eagerly rubs him down with the expensive ointment, she sneaks out of sight:

> vil drâte sî von im entweich,
> wand sî daz wol erkande
> daz schämelîchiu schande
> dem vrumen manne wê tuot,
> und barc sich durch ir höfschen muot,
> daz sî in sach und er sî niht. (ll. 3488–93)

(She walked away from him quickly because she knew quite well that the good knight would be hurt by shameful embarrassment. That is why she hid herself, so that she could see him but he could not see her.)

By keeping the newly restored Iwein unaware of his former status as the object of the female gaze, the girl clearly acts in her own and in her lady's best interest. If he knew that she had seen him naked, he would not be able to look her in the eye again; his embarrassment would be so powerful that he would flee her presence. A psychoanalytic reading of this scene suggests that ignorance of blindness/obliviousness that Freud associates with castration in this case prevents castration or loss of virility. Hence, it is not blindness that proves to be castrating, only the awareness thereof. The knight retains the ability to fight only because he is blind to his own blindness. The girl's delicate mission—namely, to recruit him for a fight against Aliers—would have failed had she not kept Iwein in the dark about his shameful exposure. Without awareness of the embarrassment there is no shame, and a "castrated" knight would be of no use to anyone. So she hides the evidence—herself—and thus protects the knight's ability to act, to effect change. Nonetheless, she continues to ogle him from her hideaway.

When Iwein comes to his senses, he begins to talk to himself. Ironically, he awakens from a dream of being well respected and dressed in "rîch gewant." During his insanity episode, his flesh and his spirit were completely separated. He had no physical awareness. While his exposed body was the defenseless object of the female gaze, his mind reveled in his former status as a powerful and dignified ruler, wrapped in beautiful clothes, shielded from the looks of others. He yearningly relives his wonderful success story in Laudine's kingdom, which he now considers a dream, something that only happened in his imagination. His separation of mind and body, his mind doing noble deeds of chivalry while his naked body becomes a sexual object, is reminiscent of Friedrich von Hausen's poem "Mîn herze und mîn lîp diu wellent scheiden" (Moser and Tervooren 81–83). The poet laments that his heart wants to stay with his lover while his body wants to go on a crusade. Iwein, on the other hand, wants to leave his body behind and return to the beautiful images unscrolling before his inner eye, the utopian vision of lost perfection.

Iwein remains the object of the female gaze—consciously, this time— during his valiant fight against Count Aliers. The lady of the castle is especially smitten with his appearance:

dô in diu graevinne enpfienc
unde engegen ime gienc
mit allen ir vrouwen,
dô mohte man schouwen
vil vriuntlîche blicke.
si besach in ofte und dicke (ll. 3791–96)

(As the countess received him and walked toward him with all her ladies one could see many friendly looks. She looked at him long and hard.)

She is so pleased with his body and his performance that she considers him worthy of taking charge of her person and her property. Her gaze fixed on him sends an unequivocal message to both Iwein and everyone else.

No words need to be exchanged; her desiring look contains both offer and promise. Iwein is not interested and declines: "sone stuont ab niender sîn muot" (l. 3800). The main difference between this and the last female gazing episode is that now the act of gazing sends a message as well. The lady gazes, the knight sees the lady gaze, and communication occurs. This mutual gaze operates within the paradigm of courtly conduct—the knight's pursuit of visible success. While the countess enjoys ogling Iwein as much as the next lady, she has a more pressing reason for bombarding him with desiring glances: she, like Laudine before her, needs a protector for her realm; otherwise, she would be "up for grabs" for the next male adventurer who happens onto her property. She communicates her wish for him to stay not only with her eyes but with her whole body—"si bat in mit gebaerden gnuoc" (l. 3819).

We have seen this type of "bodily communication attempt" before: Enite also desperately tries to make her male companion understand her without words, through gestures and glances. Neither one of these female characters is successful in conveying a message, or, more to the point, neither one of their "body talks" leads to the desired results: Enite is unable to warn Erec of approaching bandits, while the lady of Norison is unsuccessful in convincing Iwein to stay with her.

Back in the enchanted realm of Laudine, Iwein once again encounters his former ally Lunete. Lunete is incapable of recognizing him because her sight is blocked by her prison; she can only see him through a "schrunden an der tür" (l. 4020). When she retells Iwein's adventure to the "stranger" it becomes clear that Iwein had never shown any concern for her well-being. Her speech presents Arthur's court in a terrible light. Chivalry, apparently, is dead and not a single knight comes to the rescue of the damsel in distress, even though Arthur's court must have been well aware of the fact that Lunete's dire situation was caused by one of their own. Iwein is greatly moved by Lunete's version of events. He plans to help her, tie up some loose ends, and then commit suicide—right before the very eyes of his beloved Laudine:

und swenn ich iuch erloeset hân,
sô sol ich mich selben slân.
mîn vrouwe muoz doch den kampf gesehen:
wander sol vor ir geschehen. (ll. 4227–30)

(And as soon as I have freed you I will kill myself. My lady will be watching the fight, since it will happen right before her.)

Until the very end of this knight's life, the lady's gaze must witness and validate all of his pursuits. There is only one problem: Laudine has no idea that the knight who so gallantly frees Lunete and restores her honor is her own husband; curiously, Laudine does not even recognize him while carefully watching the fight; she even has a conversation with him. Iwein cannot believe it himself:

daz in diu niht erkande
diu doch sîn herze bî ir truoc,
daz was wunders genuoc. (ll. 5456–58)

(That she who carried his heart with her did not recognize him struck him as quite astonishing.)

What is the meaning of this failure of recognition? Why would no one, including Laudine, remember Iwein? Perhaps Laudine simply had not seen enough of Iwein when he left on his adventure with Gawain. She had not internalized his looks, since she did not fall in love with him by sight. There is no impression, no imprint of his physical image in her heart. Furthermore, she had never observed him in battle, and his demeanor might have changed considerably since their rushed nuptials.

Either way, it is clear that Iwein underwent a transformation—on the outside as well as on the inside. He is no longer the vain, adventure-seeking knight who turned Laudine into a widow for the thrill of it. He unselfishly—and anonymously—saved a family from an evil giant and, hours later, freed Lunete by winning an ordeal. When he arrives at the castle where three hundred young women are held captive for their labor, he sees beyond their ragged physical appearance and recognizes them for the noble ladies they are. While the old Iwein was annoyed at Laudine's expressions of grief, since they hindered his enjoyment of her as a voyeuristic object, he is now moved by the tragedy of the female group.

Iwein lost his quality as a sexually desirable object of the female gaze. After his recovery from insanity, not a single line describes his appearance, not a single female character ogles his body. He is, of course, seen and observed by ladies, but now they look at his bravery, courtesy, and martial skill, not his person. His body is now out of focus, lost in a dense fog of chivalry.

This change from a physical to a spiritual presence is underlined in Iwein's encounter with Gawain. The two men share such a strong bond that the sense of sight has become irrelevant; their knowledge of each other comes from the heart, not from the eyes: "jane wâren sî niht geste / des willen, sam der ougen" (ll. 6972–73). When they begin talking without having realized who their respective opponent is, their love for each other is coded in romantic terms:

> ichn wil mich wider iuch niht schamen,
> sprach mîn her Gâwein
> wir gehellen beide ein
>
> .   .   .   .
>
> die rede die ir habent getân
> die wold ich gesprochen hân.
> daz ir dâ minnet, daz minn ich:
> des ir dâ sorget, des sorg ich. (ll. 7430–32, 7435–38)

(I don't want to be shamed before you, said Lord Gawain, we are in agreement. . . . I wished I had said the very words that you just spoke. What you love, I also love, and what worries you worries me as well.)

Once they realize with whom they are dealing, they no longer restrain their affection. They enthusiastically begin kissing each other:

> sî freuten sich beide
> daz sî zesamne wâren komen
>
> .   .   .   .
>
> diu swert wurfen sî hin
> unde liefen ein ander an.
> ezn gelebete nie dehein man
> deheinen lieberen tac
>
> .   .   .   .
>
> sî underkusten tusentstunt
> ougen wangen unde munt. (ll. 7486–87, 7496–99, 7503–4)

(They were both overjoyed that they had found each other again. . . . They threw down their swords and ran toward each other. No one ever had a happier day. . . . They kissed each other a thousand times on the eyes, cheeks, and lips.)

According to Stephen Jaeger's argument in *Ennobling Love*, there is nothing odd about a medieval textual passage like the one above. The love between these two knights exemplifies the original courtly love, which was a public display of affection between men who admired and cherished each other. Before the mid-eleventh century, women had no part in "ennobling love" and, according to the great variety of textual evidence presented by Jaeger, this kind of affectionate behavior occurred exclusively between men.

As far as the gaze of the ladies is concerned, it seems that Iwein, in the end, regained control. His body was exposed only a short while, unbeknownst to him, at the very lowest point of his existence. After that, he deflects the female probing gaze through the unselfish way in which he serves his community. He clothed himself in an aura of knightly honor that made his body invisible, or at the very least, unrecognizable. Cloaked in an air of heroism, not even his wife recognizes him. She only knew him as a desiring subject, not as a self-sacrificing Christian warrior.

Without proposing an Iwein interpretation based on the Passion of Christ, I would like to allude to another failure of recognition, recorded in the Gospel of Luke. On the road to Emmaus, the resurrected Jesus addresses his followers, but they do not know him (Luke 24:13–35). (It is noteworthy that, in the biblical account, women knew the risen Christ by sight, while his male disciples did not.) Christ's risen body had changed in a way that his men were incapable of identifying him as their Lord. Iwein underwent a similar metamorphosis; his period of unconsciousness ended the life of the old Iwein, and the new and improved—resurrected—Iwein lived unselfishly, serving his fellow men as any good knight should.

Conclusion

Judith Bennett writes that "the power of patriarchy in our lives today rests, in part, on our failure to understand how it has worked in past times" (*Ale* 153). In the preceding chapters I offered my contribution to a better understanding of exactly how patriarchal society functioned in the European High Middle Ages, according to a broad selection of textual examples. What we can glean from those texts is that the regulation and representation of the female gaze revolves around complex psychological, sociological, and political issues.

I approached the female gaze in medieval literature from the point of view of the male psyche. In other words, examples of the female gaze in the texts I examined yielded meaning regarding the patriarchal position, internalized within individuals and externalized in the structure of society. Female desire and sexuality are seen through male eyes. Both the medieval texts and the psychoanalytic theory I applied to those texts offer a strong and relatively consistent male view of women; this perspective, in turn, aids in understanding the medieval societal system. Even though I examined the female gaze as seen from a male perspective, my research is a contribution to feminist studies.

I have, for the purposes of this study, simplified the paradigm of the gaze, discussing only the "desirable" female gaze and the "forbidden" female gaze. However, there are others that I excluded from this analysis, such as the prophetic gaze, the medical gaze, or the knowledge-acquiring gaze. The "good" female gaze serves to gratify male narcissism. We encountered this gaze in the examples provided from the courtly romances *Eneasroman*, *Parzival*, *Erec*, and *Iwein*. The approving female gaze is not about female desire but, instead, about the need of male subjects to see a positive reflection of themselves in the eyes of women. This gaze denotes inclusion; that is, it functions as a social glue, strengthening the bonds of patriarchal society. Women's admiration and approval of men increases the social standing of those male objects of the female gaze. In these literary representations, female characters take the place of the reflective pool of Narcissus; one might also remember the frequent symbolic association between woman and water. Men fall in love with themselves and other men, based on how they are reflected by the admiring female gaze. This benevolent gaze is also the motherly, noncritical gaze that Winnicott assigns to the "good-enough mother." As Chodorow explains, maleness has to be kept and re-earned. Men have to perform manhood—they must act like a man to be one—and every performer needs an audience. A little boy's period of simple sureness is short; he has to keep working at becoming and being a man. According to Simone de Beauvoir, this is the crux of the patriarchal system. Men's doing becomes their transcendence: "C'est en faisant qu'il se fait être" (30). While girls remain restricted in their immanence, men become artists, creators, adventurers; they have ambitious projects and, eventually, gain positions of power and authority over women.

We see examples of the other female gaze, the non-desirable kind, in the admonitions and warnings against it by conduct writers, such as Thomasin von Zerclaere, Der Renner, Heinrich von Melk, and Der Stricker. The non-maternal, critical female gaze works against patriarchal *ordo* and had to be ardently condemned.

Theorizing the curious effect the female desiring gaze has on women in medieval discourse means revisiting the usual suspect: misogyny. In medieval thought men represented the mind, while women were equated with the body and its sensual perception. This strict division of the sexes into two opposing groups is already found in Aristotle's *De Generatione Animalium*, where he explains how women are "matter" and men are "form." The gaze, in medieval understanding, had to be female, since women represented the senses; gazing, of course, is a sensual activity. Also, spending time "looking" as a passive female pursuit is neatly juxtaposed to male "doing" or "achieving," such as fighting or ruling.

This medieval clerical viewpoint is logically flawed as it contradicts other tenets of misogynist thought, such as the ominous danger of female beauty. How could men gaze longingly at women, or anything else for that matter, without in some way engaging in passive, sensual, that is, female-coded behavior? And why would medieval sermons again and again contain warnings to men regarding the "devil's snares" of the beautiful female body, if the temptation were not rooted in male sensuality, male sexual gazing? This is the paradox of the gaze as a medieval concept: the male is the strong, active sex, but sexual, sensual gazing is feared to be female, and hence the root of all evil. Eve gazed at the forbidden fruit and desired it. The consequence of the first female's scopophilia was the downfall of the human race.

Yet, who raises girls and boys? Women do. It is a cultural universal that young children are socialized almost exclusively by females; even in our day, male caregivers are the exception, not the rule. Hence, patriarchal values that disadvantage women are also preserved and propagated by women.

Furthermore, sociological and anthropological findings agree that in highly developed, gender-differentiated societal forms such as patriarchy, boys are more demanding and attention-seeking than girls. This phenomenon is explained by the fact that boys, unlike girls, often do not have a well-defined role in the household. Girls identify with their mother; they are from the beginning exposed to femaleness, that is, to the socially acceptable ways in which women behave and act. In many cultures, girls are seamlessly socialized into their later roles as mothers, caregivers, cooks, and so forth, while boys have little or no exposure to the work of their fathers. Since the father is often invisible, boys identify with a fantasized masculine role. They define their gender identity negatively, that is, as "not-female." Male narcissism is stronger in societies in which boys spend their earlier years exclusively with women. Since they have no clear vision of what their position in society—in "reality"—will be, they focus on their own pleasure; they remain in a state of primal narcissism. The main impact of this male self-centeredness on women is that it denies them subjectivity. This objectification is initially directed against the mother, but later it is expanded to women in general. Chodorow concludes that we can only envision narcissistic union and the complete satisfaction of pre-genital demands as progressive social principles if it is assumed that the mother is an object, not a subject. Primal narcissism, of course, is a step in human development that should be overcome in maturity. Simply put, something went wrong if the male subject "gets stuck" in the narcissistic stage and continues to see women as existing to satisfy his desires.

One explanation I offered in this book draws on object-relations theory, focusing on the pre-oedipal phase neglected or underestimated by Freud. Winnicott argues that childhood narcissism is a developmental step; a normal adult will have outgrown it. Consequently, male adult narcissism points to the fact that this healthy development was obstructed in some way, that needs were not met in the pre-oedipal phase during which the subject should have moved beyond primal narcissism. Only object-relations theory accounts for the extremely difficult path a boy has to walk on his way to becoming a man; following from the almost universal fact that his primal attachment is to the mother/female caregiver, it is the attainment of masculinity, not femininity (as Freud mistakenly thought), that is problematic. Answers lie in early childhood and the boy's relationship to his mother and/or other female caregivers, not in the later oedipal period. It is this primal relationship in the early developmental phase that is most crucial in the formation of schemata that later determine interpersonal relations.

Both adoration and vilification are ways in which men deal with the fear of the feminine. That dread and the varied strategies to deal with it are both internalized in the male psyche and externally manifested in patriarchal society. As we have seen in the medieval texts, images abound of vile, terrifying, and magically powerful female creatures like the Gorgons, the Amazons, and witches, juxtaposed to immaculate women like the Virgin, Cinderella, Condwiramurs, Griselda, and other maternal martyrs. The primary purpose of containing and regulating the gaze of women, as seen in the examples of conduct and romance literature, was to prevent women from taking charge of their own sexuality; this emancipation, of course, is the main goal of the feminist movement.

Appendix: Translations

"Remember Death" by Heinrich von Melk

Translation based on the Middle High German text *Heinrich von Melk: Von des todes gehugde*, edited by Thomas Bein and Trude Ehlert (Stuttgart: Reclam, 1994).

Profound devotion to my faith
compels me to preach to you
of looming death.
I hope most ardently
5 that I can make plain
to you worldly people
the menace and the tribulations
of death
which we all share,
10 but are sorely unprepared to face.
The prophet proclaims that
"Omnes declinaverunt"
which means that we have all
   turned away,
all have fallen away
15 from God and are headed toward
   eternal damnation.
He is right to address every man,
for among a thousand miscreants
not one can be found
who is righteous.
20 Woe, day after day, we hear
of people sinning against God!

We no longer hear of men
staying in some enclosure,
making amends there for their
   sins
25 or atoning for them elsewhere,
as did sweet Mary
who, after Christ's ascension,
despised worldly life
from a dreadful desert
30 where she was determined to
   remain,
removed from the brethren
whom, after our Lord Christ,
she never wanted to see again,
since she could never again lay
   eyes on Him.
35 Woe to you, miserable priests,
charged with leading the flock
toward heavenly bliss!
How keenly they will recoil
on Judgment Day
40 as if anyone could hide
from God's countenance that day!

They should be obedient
to what is written in Scripture
as to what our Lord God
    commands
45   —He threatened all
with eternal death
who do not live in accordance
    with His commandments
and, as Scripture teaches,
His Word is everlasting, and
50   they must firmly stand on the
    truth
and practice Christianity
and conduct their lives such
as they have read in Scriptures!—
or not one of them shall be saved.
55   The priesthood
is in a sorry state;
some hold the office without
    fulfilling its duties.
Sadly, they seem to care little about
winning lost souls.
60   Those in the priesthood
who have received the highest
    honor,
those who have been given the
    ring and the staff,
those who wear the most signifi-
    cant gowns,
the reason why they are called
    bishops,
65   they are the ones that trample the
    law:
Parishes, priories, and abbacies,
consecration, tithing, benefice,
these should not be for sale,
but, nonetheless, they are
    assigned
70   to those who can pay for them
    with earthly treasure.

Their disciples have taken note
    and
from their masters'
example they learned:
Confession and burial,
75   reading Mass and psalms,
these are offered up everywhere
for a price;
be it last rites or baptism
or all other services—
80   none are given freely
if they can get money for them.
Woe, on Judgment Day,
they will get their just reward!
Not one of them can hope
85   for help on that day;
a priest who has sold spiritual
    gifts—
how could his misdeeds
ever be forgiven!
If he is found guilty,
90   he will forever be bound
in the hot flames of hellfire.
His cries of regret will come too
    late,
all the good he does
while remaining in such error
95   is cursed by God;
his prayers will go unheard
and never reach God's ear.
His memory will be extinct for all
    eternity.
Those who belong to the order of
    priests
100 have the power of the twelve
    apostles,
through the Word of God which
    they preach,
to either bind sinners or deliver
    them.

They must care for them
or God will punish them, as well,
105   if they expect rewards without
         effort.
They receive, from God through
         His prophet,
a horrifying testimony:
"They swallow up the sins of my
         people."
As our Lord Himself said:
110   "They put a great burden on my
         poor people,
too heavy for them to bear,
and then make no attempt to
         lighten it."
On the other hand, many are so
         meek
that they give false comfort to the
         children of the devil,
115   thus supporting them in their
         offenses;
whoever has anything to offer to
         them
gets permission to do whatever he
         wants,
it is impossible
to be so wicked
120   that money won't fix it.
They strain out the fly
but swallow the camel.
Only the poor are rebuked,
the ones that should move them
         to pity,
125   but the actions of the mighty
are deemed sweet and righteous.
Unless God changes His words,
from one soul to another,
what shall happen to a man who
130   through his guilt,
out of greed, loses a

thousand souls or more?
What we learn from Scriptures is
that there will be great suffering
135   on Judgment Day
when, without mercy,
God's wrath will descend on
         them.
How dearly will they pay
then for those worldly riches
140   and the unholy liberties they took
in their lives without restraint!
What's more, priests are now
         clamoring
for the right
of men of the cloth
145   to take wives,
instead of ministering to the flock
         like—
to make a comparison—
a shepherd cares for his sheep
and a master for his disciples,
150   that is how they should set them-
         selves apart.
Instead, they want to live a life of
         comfort!
Why, then, were they put in posi-
         tions of leadership?
Indecency and saintliness,
debauchery and purity
155   cannot coexist.
Since the priest
handles the Eucharist,
should he not shrink
from touching women?
160   Truly, they have been led astray!
This is a tenet of our faith:
When the priest stands at the
         altar,
whispering his prayers,
the heavens are opening up

165 so that his words may penetrate.
Out of the angelic host,
the Lord sends His servants.
The offering meets with approval
and all the sins of believers
170 are blotted out,
if they have true faith.
Whosoever is officiating Mass—
how pure his heart must be!
Let us join together in lamenting
175 how displeased God must be
that Holy Mass is offered to us
by those who fail to live
or minister properly
as is their obligation.
180 This is why we should be furious
with them!
But where God's Word and the
blessed hand
work in harmony at the altar
God is present in the flesh,
through a sinner
185 and through the holiest man
who ever became a priest.
If only I dared tell you what I
know!
Those who added to their Christian vows
other vows—
190 regardless of how well they know
the Scriptures,
those who have withdrawn from
this world—
either Scripture is lying,
or they are in a horrible bind.
They should be dead to the world,
195 mortify their flesh,
so that it gradually becomes
numb while
looking up at the soul,

like a servant girl to her mistress.
Instead, they display hatred and
envy,
200 dissention and discord.
They are good at ridiculing and
gloating
and it is hard to discern
whether true love
will ever enter their hearts.
205 They talk a lot.
Position and power
is all they care about.
They only serve in plain sight,
not out of love, but out of fear.
210 They don't remain inside the walls
of the church,
they don't want to be tied down.
This is clearly visible in those
who arrange their lives around
outward appearances.
They choose their own penance
215 which they perform quite
publicly.
They may not be able to afford a
donkey
but in evil ways
with their heart and tongue
they strangely long to enrich
themselves.
220 If it were possible, through lordly
delicacies,
to enter heaven
with well-groomed beards
and smartly cut hair,
they all would be in line for
sainthood.
225 This is the reason for lay people's
suspicion:
We witness the actions of the
unfaithful priests,

and assume that the others are
   just like them.
They are the disgrace and the
   downfall
of spiritual communities.
230 What law says
   that someone becomes a lord
   by forsaking the world,
   if he was a pauper before?
   In wintertime, the grass withers,
235 though it was green throughout
   summer.
   If a man deems himself brave in
   the world,
   and decides to live a spiritual life
   where he must do battle with the
   devil
   it seems only reasonable
240 that he should convince his
   brethren
   first of all
   of his abilities.
   We purposefully addressed this
   matter
   which greatly angers
245 priests and monks.
   In the back and in the front
   they should be covered with eyes,
   so that, everywhere,
   they can recognize the enemies,
250 who are trying to approach those
   entrusted to the care of the clergy.
   If they, however, choose blindness
   they will be blinded for eternity.
   This has been revealed to us
255 in the words of Scripture:
   Where a blind man leads another,
   they will both fall into the pit.
   This parable is understood by
   most:

The pit signifies hell.
260 If you want to know who the
   blind men are:
   Those are the worthless teachers
   who lead their listeners astray,
   right down the eternal abyss.
   Yet another call shall sound forth
265 from our horn,
   which will now also anger lay
   people.
   Worldly judges
   are opponents
   of God and all that is righteous.
270 They resemble wolves:
   They stalk what they want to
   hunt.
   There is no more honor
   among lay people.
   A father cannot trust his child
275 he cannot be free of concern
   that once he is grown, today or
   tomorrow,
   he might chase his father from his
   possessions.
   If he loses everything
   and, once rich, is now poor—
280 Woe, what if no one takes pity on
   him
   among all his relatives!
   Everyone wants to enrich
   himself,
   and where there is nothing to
   gain,
   there is no longer any value
285 in kinship.
   Neither the lord of his servant
   nor the servant of his lord
   can expect faithfulness and
   honor.
   Knights and ladies

290 have a way of life, as we will show,
   which is abhorrent to God.
   All their thoughts revolve around
   inventing new fashions,
   destroying their souls in the
      process.
295 This is the very trap of pride
   which once even ensnared the
      devil.
   Nothing is as appealing to him as
   snatching us away from God's
      protection by
   seducing us with the same vice.
300 The sins of pride are the gravest
   among those committed against
      God's grace.
   The proud man is the son of the
      devil.
   Whenever the devil ensnares a
      man through pride,
   he has already vanquished him.
305 This is confirmed in the book of
      Job.
   There, it says that the devil is
   the prince over all children of
      pride.
   God help us all so
   that we do not join the one
310 who brought pride into the world.
   It is the root of all evil;
   it hinders the Holy Spirit
   from dwelling in us.
   We must flee this wickedness
315 because it keeps us from acting in
      a spiritual way.
   Pride is the leprosy of the soul.
   Women are most afflicted with it,
   and I am not even speaking of
      noble ladies.
   In the alleys and in the churches,

320 everywhere we see the poor
      female day laborer
   who can barely support herself;
      yet,
   she cannot be happy unless
   she makes her dress so long
   that the folds drag along the
      ground
325 stirring up the dust as she walks by,
   as if this brought change to her
      situation!
   With her prideful gait
   and with artificial color on her
      cheeks
   with yellow ribbons
330 peasant girls everywhere want to
      pretend
   to be equal to the daughters of
      noblemen,
   primping and fussing
   with their dresses.
   Truly disgusted with this behavior
      are those
335 who care for the proper order of
      things.
   Whatever it is that someone
      thinks up,
   the others are quick to covet the
      same.
   Not much is left of the rightful
      order of things
   throughout all layers of society.
340 God cannot be happy with this.
   We do not intend to speak ill of
      noble ladies,
   but we cannot be silent on the
      behavior of knights.
   Pride has two companions
   which expose knights to the red-
      hot sparks

345 of the eternal fire.
He owes God gratitude
who lives without them,
who resisted haughtiness,
because that is how knights are
often led astray,
350 tied up by the ropes of eternal
death
thus losing their lives.
After that, the time for salvation
has passed:
damnation is his lot.
Wherever knights gather,
355 they take turns bragging
about their whoring.
They cannot keep their shame to
themselves
but, instead, take pride in their
whoremongering.
If there is one among them who
cannot hold his own,
360 he feels inferior
among his peers.
Wherever some are assembled
to talk about manly valor
it is most rarely brought up
365 how much strength is required of
the one
who must do battle against the
devil.
They always bring up things
that have no connection to the
matter at hand.
Then they bring even more shame
on themselves
370 when they say things like: All
through the land,
this man has earned our respect
because he has done a lot of
killing.

The prophet clearly teaches this:
They rejoice because in all things
375 they do the most evil
of which they are capable.
Those to whom these words
apply,
these braggarts,
are guilty of turning our world,
380 sadly, into a faithless one.
Rightfully we mourn
the loss of excellent men
of bygone times.
When this world has reached its
end,
385 woe to the last of our heirs!
How rough it will be for them,
before God and Christendom!
Where today is the wisdom of our
forefathers,
which is no longer fully known
390 by their descendants?
All of those living in these times
use their minds
to deceive one another,
to ridicule, and cheat each other.
395 Today's youth is rotten to the
core.
Honor, discipline, and virtue,
all rolling down hill like a wheel.
Rome, the capital of the world,
no longer has a father like she
used to.
400 There, one may expect
neither justice nor mercy,
just plotting how to get to riches.
The powerful man is of noble
birth
and eats at the table of princes.
405 He is wise and strong,
he is handsome and smart,

and praiseworthy all through the
land.
The weak man is not thought of
well.
Higher clergy
410 should be called rulers
rather than teachers.
If they own a lot of shields,
helmets, and armor,
their joy consists of
415 riding with a group,
taking possession of the land,
caring little who owns it;
their charges longing to be free
to do whatever they want.
420 The mighty are living high off the
hog,
while the poor are reduced to
begging;
this is not found in Scripture.
Clergymen are greedy,
peasants are envious,
425 merchants are untrustworthy,
and there is no chastity among
women.
Ladies and knights
do not need to argue about
who leads the better life.
430 Their vassals want to be free.
The good and the righteous
are outnumbered by thousands
of those who have no witnesses
testifying to their integrity.
435 Now I have said so much more
than was my intention
when I began to write this poem.
May no one resent me
for speaking the truth.
440 If I left the boundaries
of my initial subject matter

it is because of the dire situation
and the deceitful nature of this
life
which distracts us in many ways
445 from reflecting upon it,
as we have shown.
Here, we want to end this section
of the speech,
the preceding words do not
correspond
to what follows:
450 "Of everyday life"
could be the title of that part.
What we want to say about death
you will find written below.
We will now begin in the name of
the Lord.
455 Now, remember your death
with the words of lord Job,
he says: "Short are my days,
my life is approaching the grave."
In another passage, he made a
similar point:
460 "Remember your creator in your
youth,
before time takes its toll,
wearing you out,
before the dust that you are
returns to the earth."
465 The following words
also make the same point:
"My life is like a wind,
like a stream that flows by,
I am like ash;
470 my likeness is ash, and flue ash."
These words are a weak
consolation,
which was also spoken by another
prophet.
He says, "My life is like grass

which is dry today but was green
yesterday."
475 This is how we recognize the wise
man:
He never forgets that he must die.
We are also admonished by Solo-
mon's writing;
he says, "Son, never forget
your last hour!
480 Then you will live without sin."
Woe to the man who delays his
salvation and confession
until his dying day!
Wretched man, brittle clay!
The two will be reunited.
485 Just as you first came into
existence
before your mother brought you
forth
with pains and lamentations,
with great discomfort,
when you owned nothing
490 but your skin and bones.
You were born without clothes;
why are you so obsessed with
meaningless gains?
Even if God's order
495 were to estrange you from the
whole world,
he still gave you a shirt
to cover your shame.
You do not spend a single night
on this earth
without the chance that you
might die.
500 Long before you can signal your
state
with wailing,
you have made it clear
that you are a miserable wretch.

When your last hour has arrived,
505 you will cry out repeatedly.
This is the order of things, that he
who dies in pain
was born in pain,
as is shown by the first scream
after birth,
510 the wailing of the newborn child.
We will speak to you of the son of
a king
to see whether you can discern
if he was born
to suffer and to hurt
515 or to rejoice and be well.
There are many unfortunate
things
we should better leave alone
which might cause a boy
to gravely fall ill.
520 Let's assume his becoming a
knight
to be a joyous occasion.
He is not going to enjoy it for
long.
All too soon he will have to labor;
evenings and mornings
525 building his wretched reputation,
namely, today and tomorrow,
working on
expanding his fief.
He surely cannot even rely
on the full fealty or the gratitude
530 of his closest relatives.
If he chooses a comfortable life
he quickly loses his good
reputation,
and he is shunned
by his equals.
535 If, however, he decides to forgo
his obligations

his soul cannot be saved.
No matter what he decides to do,
failure is the likeliest outcome!
He worries day and night
540 that someone might betray him
or poison him.
That happens more often than I
or anyone else can tell you.
We cannot conceal from you all
the sufferings
545 that afflict both the powerless and
the mighty
in manifold ways.
One has the fever, or the gout,
another loses his hearing or his
sight;
another loses a limb;
550 yet another is so deformed
that he can neither walk nor
stand;
another loses his sense of smell or
taste;
another loses his speech.
Such horrible things
555 could afflict any man—
can anyone talk his way out of
them,
powerful and noble as he might
be,
can he prevent such illnesses?
Let's assume that someone could,
560 completely without pain,
arrive at his last day,
even though that is hardly
possible—
well, what happens then?
As soon as the wretched soul
565 leaves the body,
look, brother, how he just lies
there.

Even if he had dominion over
three kingdoms,
his burial plot is the same size as
that of a beggar.
570 Some we see stretched out,
covered with precious blankets,
encircled by many candles,
myrrh and incense
also burning there.
575 And if it happens
that the funeral lasts longer than
expected,
and the friends of the departed
are all assembled,
they are concerned with
580 burying him in splendor.
Woe to all this corrupting power,
when the devilish forces of hell
mightily swallow up the wretched
soul!
What difference does it make
585 where the miserable bones are
buried
if the pitiful soul is denied
communion with all the saints?
Woe to the night when he is
resurrected!
Let's assume for a moment
590 that the funeral banquet
lasts two or three days
or even longer:
It is still a miserable departure!
Nothing that ever was born
595 ends up more vile
and repulsive to this world.
Now, beautiful wife, why don't
you walk over there
to your beloved husband and gaze
at him
and look carefully

600 at his face,
at the part of his hair,
at the way his hair is smoothed
  down!
Look closely
whether his demeanor is still as
  joyful
605 as when he openly and tenderly
looked at you.
Now look, where are his flattering
  glances
which used to feed
the pride of ladies?
610 Now look at the way
his tongue is lying in his mouth,
with which he was able to sing
  love songs
so sweetly!
Now it can bring forth
615 neither words nor tunes.
Now look, what has become of
  the chin
with the stylish beard?
Now look, how miserable
the arms and the hands are
  positioned,
620 with which he used to
touch and hold you!
Where are his feet, with which he
pranced around beside the ladies
  in such a courtly manner?
You used to ogle him from behind,
625 admiring the way the tights
  hugged his legs;
sadly, they are not so closely fitted
now, are they!
Now he is completely unfamiliar
  to you,
the one you used to adorn with
silken strings

threaded into his shirt at different
  places.
630 Now, look at his middle:
he is inflated like a sail.
Foul stench and vapors
are wafting up from under his
  shroud
and won't allow him
635 to dwell above ground with you
  much longer.
Woe, this deplorable process of
  dying
the worst part of death,
reminds you, man, of your
  transience.
Now prepare yourself
640 before your last hour,
which was always looming,
  catches up with you:
"Repentina calamitas,"
which means: get ready for such a
  death
and say, just like Job:
645 "My years are fleeting.
Truly, I am walking a path on
  which
I shall never return."
Before your bed
turns into your death bed,
650 turn your ship around,
so that, in the middle of the
  ocean,
the southern winds won't toss you
  to and fro
and you can no longer
steer it safely toward the harbor.
655 Once you are in the grip of illness
you lose the ability to sin anyway.
Sins will leave you, not the other
  way around.

Now tell me, wretched brother,
why
do you want to see a priest then?
660 How can you get your affairs in
order then,
when it's too late to repent?
You waited too long to change
your ways.
You mighty and noble young
man,
go, have a look at something
ghastly
665 and approach the crypt of your
father:
open his coffin
and have a look at his remains,
moan and cry.
If you feel like it, you can say the
following—
670 it won't hurt your reputation—
"Dear father and lord,
tell me what's become of you.
I see your corpse rotting,
it has almost completely turned
into dirt.
675 Disgusting worms are crawling
around in it.
The stench of your grave
numbs my senses,
the odor is horrible.
My heart is heavy
680 because you were so handsome
and disappeared so soon."
It is the sad order of things:
What blooms like a lily
becomes like a garment
685 gnawed and eaten by moths.
Whosoever forgets this is lost.
Perhaps you would have found
the right words

if you had been moved by grief
over the loss of your beloved
father.
690 Just think about
how he would answer you
if the order of nature allowed it
or if God granted it.
I don't want to speak too long
695 but I speak for him and with him;
listen carefully:
"I want to give you, dear son,
an answer to your question.
My situation is hopeless.
700 The cruelty I experience
is inescapable
and I suffer it every day anew.
Fire and darkness surround me,
right and left,
705 above and below.
If someone found a written account of my torment,
his reading of it would be
everlasting.
This is my lament to you, dear son.
But what use should you have of
my long speech?
710 The chains of God's wrath
have bound me permanently.
I have received my bitter reward
for everything I have done
for which I did not repent, leading to my perdition.
715 I knew no moderation
in drinking and eating;
now I am overcome
by thirst and by hunger.
My flesh used to burn
720 in the heat of passion;
now I am being scorched by the
punishment of God

in a fire that no one can ever
  extinguish.
I suffer pain and distress.
If only I had never been born!
725 Greed and pride,
  those two have locked me up
  behind the doors of hell.
Waves of black tar surround me
  here,
  along with flames of hot fire.
730 I hear the gnashing of teeth,
  cries and lamentations;
  shouts of agony
  from those who have no hope
  of being delivered
735 from this abyss.
Oh, why did I ever do the things
  that caused me to be in their
    company!
If only there were mercy for me,
  and I were spared
740 from meeting the devil,
  from facing him,
  how glad I would be!
My lament comes too late.
But I advise you, dear son,
745 to be mindful of my example
  and not accede to the world as I
    did;
  if you do not remember my
    torment
  you will suffer the same fate.
Tell me now, dear son,
750 what good are my wealth
  and my ill-gotten riches?
My great cleverness
I wanted to show off through
  the purchase of fiefs and property,
755 castles, manors, hides of land,
  and other lordly possessions.

This is the reason why I had to
  relinquish my soul.
How have you shared the wealth
  with me,
  since I departed from you?
760 Hardly at all!
Where are the alms that you
  handed out?
Where are the needy whom you
  comforted?
When have you had Mass read in
  remembrance of my soul?
You have forgotten me
765 as if I had never been born.
To think that I took up
  this burden for you,
  which is the reason why I am now
    detested
  by the righteous judge!
770 Cursed be the day of my birth!
Whatever I took,
  remorselessly,
  from widows and orphans,
  is now the cause of my torment.
775 Now look, my dear son,
  if you know what is good for you,
  and remember how my cleverness
    guided me
  and enabled me
  to make you wealthy and lordly
780 while I am suffering in fear and
    pain.
You are sitting down before an
  opulent feast
while I, unfortunately, am in the
  grip of the devil.
You are famous throughout the
  land,
all the while I must endure great
  infamy.

785 But my condemnation would not
      be so severe
    were it not for the wealth I ac-
      cumulated for you,
    which you are now using to fund
      your wicked life.
    No matter how much you rebel
      against God,
    your last day arrives like a thief in
      the night;
790 your wealth will not buy you a
      delay.
    Would you like to know now
      where I am asking you to go?
    To the place where, from one day
      to the next,
    you could fall into the deepest
      abyss.
    Decide to repent!
795 As far as my own flesh is
      concerned,
    I am making the ominous predic-
      tion, that
    when I return to it on Judgment
      Day, it will,
    along with my wretched soul,
    go to a life which is death.
800 What a high price to pay for
      all I ever enjoyed.
    Oh, if only I had never seen the
      light of day!
    His retribution
    can never be adequately
805 described by any tongue.
    That I am now without hope
    to ever see God,
    except for the day on which He
      judges me.
    Even if this were my only
      torment,

810 it would be my eternal death.
    Repent while there's still time, my
      dear child!"
    When out of all who are covetous
      in this world
    only one saves his soul, it's a
      miracle.
    Eternal damnation awaits them,
815 along with the one
    who is tied up
    with the chains of his avarice;
    they will burn throughout
      eternity
    in the horrific flames of the fire.
820 Woe, if anyone knew of the great
      agony
    that is the lot of the wealthy,
    he would always steer clear of
      worldly possessions.
    Whosoever is found with an ac-
      cumulation of riches,
    gathered together through greed,
825 is barred from entering into
      heaven.
    Thus, he has made poor use
    of the wealth he accumulated;
    just as the Son of God
      forewarned:
    He clearly said that
830 it is easier for a camel
    to pass through the eye of a
      needle
    than for a rich man to sit in Abra-
      ham's lap.
    If a rich man thinks he can be
      saved,
    he should ask the priests what
      they read in Scripture:
835 he has nothing, yet possesses all
      things;

he does not need to be asked by
    anyone
whether he should share his
    wealth;
he lets anyone partake of it
who asks, in the name of God.
840 Saint Paul, the apostle, says
that striving for wealth
is idolatry.
We can clearly see it in the
    greedy:
In the place of their Creator
845 they put what He created.
Be it gold, silver, or clothing
or any other venal thing,
it all has to be left behind.
Like a thief the last day will sneak
    up on you;
850 your possessions will offer no
    protection,
you have to leave all of it behind.
Then your repentance is
    incomplete
and your confession will be of
    little use to you.
It can easily happen,
855 even if you have avoided thinking
    about it,
that death seizes us unexpectedly,
how gladly you would like to act
    then, but you can't!
As long as God grants you the
    ability
to choose between two things,
860 whatever good works you carry
    out,
a penny given is more useful
for your soul
than a thousand pounds left after
    your death.

And don't save it for your wife!
865 There are few who are
    trustworthy;
most are fickle and unstable.
And don't sin against God be-
    cause of your children!
Their lives are also fleeting,
they are not virtuous, but
870 inclined toward depravity,
and disobedient.
However, if you train them in
    righteousness,
your effort will not be in vain.
I have much to say to you on the
    subject,
875 but I have to remain silent.
If you wish to avoid a great
    misfortune,
repent in time!
Woe, how little forgiveness you
    will receive
if you are counting on the mercy
    of hell.
880 God forbid that you are ever sent
    there!
The threat of such words,
wretched brother, you must fear
    greatly
and understand well, remembering
what, one day, might happen to
    you.
885 And now tell me, brother, who
    you are!
As if Christ, our Lord,
was speaking to you,
and spoke with His own mouth:
"You, whom I have loved most
    among my creation
890 why have you rejected the
    teachings

of my apostles
which invited you to heaven?
If you do not want to make an
    effort,
even though I have given so much
895 to earn back heaven for you
you will not partake of it,
if you prefer to live in sin
and remain in disobedience,
just like your ancestors.
900 Fear nothing more than
being condemned
to hell for this.
Do you not regard this as a great
    shame?
Never again will you see me,
905 if the pleasures of this world,
which no one can enjoy for long,
are more important to you than
    heavenly glory.
I will say no more:
You will not partake of it;
910 fear no other calamity."
If you have listened to these words,
keep them in your heart
and consider it foolish talk
that the devil and hell
915 cannot harm us in the next life.
What joy is left for the one
who will never see God?
When will he be delivered from
    damnation
after he was set apart from the
    one
920 without whom there is no joy?
Let us no longer speak of the
    great torment
that looms over the condemned,
which they will suffer in hell,
let us not mention it again.

925 What could possibly be worse
than never seeing God?
He to whom this happens is born
    cursed,
like the one who endures God's
    wrath
and His judgment.
930 Whosoever stained himself
with manifold sins,
should the devil not bind him,
and cast him into eternal misery,
from where he will always and
    without end
935 call out his lamentations,
where the one who seduced him
    stands over him,
in his ghastly shape,
where the inexhaustible fountains
rise up from the abyss
940 and where he will see the flowing
rivers of bubbling tar,
the crackling pyres
and, on the other side,
the growing masses of ice in hell;
945 even if a hundred burning
    mountains
were there, as well,
they could not melt it,
even if the devils with their fiery
    claws
stirred up a mighty storm.
950 Verily, it is a horrible house of ice!
You haughty ones will get your
    just reward there:
your iniquity will be punished.
Those among you who are
    whoremongers,
just try to protect yourself
955 with your deceit and your
    cunning.

You orators will be silenced,
and you get the punishment you
    deserve;
just pull your swords
and defend yourselves, if you can!
960 You slanderers will be silenced;
the only redress you will have left
are curses.
Murderers will see
how they can be struck down
    without a sword.
965 There, they will scream and moan
but they will still have to submit
    to the devil's power.
Thieves and robbers—
how incredulous they would be,
if someone told them about their
    fate
970 of how, one day, they will be
    forced to drink
hot waves of tar!
It is immensely unwise
to refuse to ponder this:
he will forever be trapped
975 in the dungeon of eternal torment
from which there is no escape,
as we have already said.
Even if the devil lost his
    dominion
so that he could no longer harm us,
980 we should be moved by love
to aspire to the highest heaven
and should heave a daily sigh
from this wretched valley of tears
toward the heavenly hall.
985 All lament is unknown
among the heavenly host.
All thought is freed there,
no one there knows what fear is;
they can tell more tales of joy

990 than anyone has ever heard or
    seen here
or is capable of imagining.
Their greatest bliss
is the sight of God:
No one ever tires of this joy
995 and this peace without ambush,
grace without disgrace.
Their joy is never ending.
There is so much bliss there
that it is indescribable with
    words.
1000 A thousand years are like one
    day.
Blessed and wise is the one
who remembers the eternal
    paradise
which is our inheritance.
Oh, how he despises
1005 the things of this world!
To him they mean no more than
    a heap of dung.
He is fully aware
that the benevolence of God
with great wisdom
1010 has created, according to His
    divine plan,
a dwelling for His saints.
Also, it is clearly written
that paradise is located on this
    earth
surrounded by tall mountains
1015 sheltering it from view;
there, God has hidden the secret
    signs
for those whom He loves.
This domain is free from all care,
but high regard in heaven
1020 is even more praiseworthy;
    if all people

who were ever born
wanted to speak
of the grace
1025 which is in heaven
not even the smallest part of it
could be known to us.
Blessed are those who strive for
  it with all their might!
Lead to this place, dear God,
1030 through the grace of your mother,
and through the prayer of all
  your saints,
your humble and sinful servant
  Heinrich.

Also, bless the Abbott Erkenfried
and keep him, Lord, in your
  peace,
1035 as well as all who trust
that we will live with you one
  day
in heaven
and that we will, daily
with all angels,
1040 in the Holy Spirit
praise the Father and the Son
in saecula saeculorum
Amen.

"The Walled-In Woman," by Der Stricker

Translation based on the Middle High German text *Die eingemauerte Frau*, edited by Otfrid Ehrismann (Stuttgart: Reclam, 1992).

A highly virtuous knight
took a woman in marriage,
but she wanted to have her own way
instead of obeying his will.
5 He would not stand for it
and told her to give up.
However, since neither pleading nor praying
helped to make her behave better
he threatened her greatly,
10 but she threatened him right back.
He hit her with his fist
and said: "Now I care as little about the sack
as I care about the sackrope."
He tore her dress and
15 he took up a heavy club
and let her feel his anger.
He beat her so long
with force and haste
that his arm was sore
20 and he did not feel up to hitting her any longer.
He had severely injured her on one side
where there was nothing left to see
but broken skin and blood.
He said: "Are you going to be obedient from now on?"

25 She said: "What's the rush?
God knows I have a ways to go.
You may have to wait a good while,
especially since three sides of my body are still
untouched and unbeaten."
30 He said: "God knows I deeply regret
that I stupidly
lost my composure because of you."
She said: "You'll kill yourself,
unless I die soon."
35 She predicted great losses for him.
He then commanded that a brick enclosure be built
without a door,
but with an opening for a window.
There, she was walled in.
40 He said: "Since you soured
on my friendship and my service
you shall be rid of me.
You may be able to recover better
and should be happy without me.
45 Since you appear to hate me so much,
this will be best for both of us.

It will be a good way to avoid
  anger."
The blackest bread
that he could find,
50 the kind that was usually thrown
  before his dogs,
was now given to her.
She had to live off the worst
  scraps
that could be found about the
  house.
Yet, he had a greater punishment
  in store for her:
55 he simply remained silent when
  she spoke to him.
He also made sure to sit where
  she could watch him,
during his pleasure time and his
  meals.
He had a positive influence on his
  servants,
easing their burdens.
60 He always placed a lovely woman
  next to himself.
Fine wools and velvet,
the best materials money could
  buy
this woman wore in her daily life.
65 He held her and kissed her
whenever he felt like it
while his wife was watching.
If she suffered because of that
the master did not care.
70 He was pleased with himself all
  the time and
everybody else approved of his
  measures, as well.
His godly behavior even convinced
his wife's own relatives not to op-
  pose him.

It was clearly preferable to be on
  good terms with him
75 than to have him for an enemy.
He remained so steadfast in his
  position
that his wife nearly despaired.
When she complained to her kin
about the imprisonment and the
  shame
80 and the hardship she had to suffer
they said to her: "We know exactly how
full of evil you are and
that he is justified in dealing with
  you in this way.
You have a wicked heart
85 and this is the reward you get for it.
It serves you right."
And when she was able to convince one relative
to take up her case before her
  husband
he was told by him:
90 "I am delighted that you came to
  me in this matter.
I will gladly follow your request
  and your counsel
if you put your money where
  your mouth is.
If she decides to return to her old
  wickedness,
everything you own will be mine.
95 Under this condition only, I will
  set her free.
I'll even put her in charge of
  everything I own."
"No, thank you," her relative
  quickly said.
"I am well aware of her nasty
  disposition.

I am not willing to risk everything on this bet."
100 In this way, her relatives
  stopped pleading for her.
Afterwards, he was quite gracious
  toward them.
He offered them great honor
and endeared himself to them,
105 with goodness and with love.
That is how he separated his wife
from all her kin.
Then she found herself completely alone.
The lady was told
110 that everyone was silent
who had come to help her and
that they did not want to help her
  anymore.
When she heard the sad news
that she would never be freed,
115 even the devils that had possessed
  her
fled from her.
The Holy Spirit came
and kept her company.
Her great evil simply vanished
120 and her pride quickly fell off her.
Her vicious and evil disposition
just melted away and she became
  righteous
and she began regretting her sin
from the bottom of her heart.
125 She sent for a priest
to get her affairs in order
so that, if her body died,
her soul might not perish.
When she saw the priest
130 she knelt down before him and
  said:
"I am the most sinful woman

that ever walked the earth.
I regret that so bitterly.
Through the power of the Holy
  Spirit
135 offer me now your help and advice as to
what I can do that my evil deeds
against God will be forgiven,
so that my soul will not perish."
He said: "I can only advise you of
  one thing.
140 If you are concerned with your
  soul
and with everlasting life
you must become an excellent
  wife!
The best advice for you is
that you should cast off all evil
145 that separates you both from God
and from those others
who have your best interest at
  heart."
She said: "My evil heart
has been changed by God.
150 I want to obey all his
  commandments,
wherever I can.
In the name of God, ask my
  husband
that he may give me his affections
and that he allow me, while I live,
155 to pay for my sins right here,
all the while seeking God's grace.
I feared neither God nor my
  husband
and this is how I forfeited the
  world.
I shall never approach it again.
160 The devil had taken from me
both fear and love,

wisdom and good judgment.
I don't know what I did to so offend God
that He gave the devil
165 such enormous powers over me.
I truly don't know what I did
wrong.
The only thing I know for sure is
that I must have acted worse than
wicked;
I will always be torn up with grief
about that.
170 Since my husband did not take
my life,
he treated me far better
than I ever treated him.
I am now in your charge
as you answer to God.
175 So prove your loyalty to me
and allow me to put myself in
your care."
The priest immediately went
to find the husband alone.
He said: "Now, do as I bid you,
180 You will thereby win God's grace,
whatever my lady did to you,
forgive her for it.
From now on she will do nothing
other than what you wish.
185 If you are not willing to believe
her,
then take my word for it.
She has deeply repented of her sin,
and she is now asking for your
grace.
She is not just saying it
190 so that you should improve her
situation.
She does it for the salvation of her
soul.

You have been harboring great
anger against her—
let go of it.
If you are trying to please God
195 and to gain eternal life,
then prove it with your action
toward your wife."
The master of the house said: "Let
us go over to her,
so that I may find out the truth,
whether she is worthy of good
treatment
200 which I will then readily grant
her."
They walked over to the window.
There crouched the woman before him,
on her knees, and said:
"That I ever opposed you like
that,
205 I will regret forever.
Through my unholy behavior
I have lost God, the world, and
you.
For the love of God, let go of your
rage.
God will help us both much more
readily this way.
210 I brought God's anger on myself,
and I will always suffer because
of it.
I do not deserve
God's incredible goodness.
Now, my lord, have mercy on me
215 and forgive me so that God may
forgive you.
Allow me, as long as I live,
to remain here, seeking God's
grace,
for the sake of both our sins."

Her husband was well pleased
    with that speech
220 and his heart was filled with
        delight.
    Quickly, he let that joy shine
        through.
    He sent for her kin, and for his
        own, as well,
    so that they rushed over
    and brought their wives with them.
225 When they had all come
    with happiness and joyful noise,
    he welcomed them cheerfully and
        said:
    "Because of the punishment I
        gave to my wife,
    God turned her around.
230 Whosoever will honor her for
        that,
    will also win my favor.
    And everyone who is well dis-
        posed toward me
    should rejoice with me now
    since I will reconcile with her."
235 And, right away, they requested
        and were granted
    that the wall be torn down.
    She was told to come out.
    She asked, in the name of God, to
        be allowed to stay,
    yet again opposing herself to his
        will.
240 The priest went to her
    and ordered her to be obedient
    if she loved the name of Christ.
    By being obedient to her husband
    she would be doing God's will.
245 She was lectured about the truth
    so long and so extensively
    that she finally came out.

He now asked her to forgive all
        her suffering
    that he had caused her.
250 That was also the prayer of all
        those
    who had come to see her that day
    when they had received the
        invitation.
    She said: "Whatever wrong you
        committed against me
    I will gladly absolve you of it;
255 you are innocent toward me;
    alas, I am the guilty one,
    I shall never recover from it,
    I would have well deserved to die.
    May God grant me penitence.
260 Since you don't permit me to
        remain behind the wall
    to pacify God's indignation,
    at least, allow me
    to honor God
    through turning around other
        evil wives.
265 I am capable of doing that now."
    Both laymen and priests
    fell to her feet.
    They desired the same atonement
    that she had received from the
        all-powerful God.
270 She said: "Truly, I want you to
        know
    that I am capable of driving out
        the evil
    from wicked women.
    I know full well where they are
        coming from.
    Whosoever has a wicked wife,
275 verily, entrust her to me,
    I will take care of transforming
        her

I will make her turn away from
   her evil ways,
and she will become like me.
God has shown his favor to me.
280 I know that she who entrusts
   herself to me
will become right good,
and will be happy to act properly
   from then on."
All the knights who were present
were well pleased with that offer.
285 They said: "You, lady, are a saint.
May God grant that your soul and
   body
won't be separated for a long time
   to come."
Quite a few among them said:
   "My wife
has put me through so much
   suffering
290 that she must quickly be brought
   before you
so that you can turn her around
   for me."
There was laughter all around
by knights, as well as by ladies.
They were all shown by the lord
   of the house
295 that he wanted them to have a
   great time
and whatever it took,
food, entertainment, and music,
there was more than plenty of all
   that.
Thus, he honored his wife.
300 All the virtuous behavior
which one expects from a lady,
and which, in a seemly woman
amounts to great praise,

the lady of the house was now
   filled with it.
305 She began to please all people
so perfectly well
that everyone confirmed
who heard and saw her
that she gave great honor to God.
310 The world was beautifully
   crowned
with her virtues
well decorated and embellished.
The festivities lasted seven days.
After that, complaints were heard
315 that they should not have ended
   so soon.
When the time came to say
   good-bye,
the lady stepped up on a bench.
She spoke: "Now thank your host
that he has been merciful to me,
320 and that he has glorified God and
   himself
in his behavior toward me.
I have committed grave injustice
against him
and I would have done even
   worse things
325 had he not hindered me
in the way of the wise and the
   brave.
No matter how much he honors
   me now,
I am still deeply in his debt.
The more he trusts
330 and honors me now,
the greater is my regret
that I committed such heinous
   treachery
against God and against him.

Now, reveal me to the world
335 and make known my repentance
everywhere in the land
and be trustworthy about spread-
  ing the word:
be he poor or rich
whosoever brings his wicked wife
  before me,
340 her burden will be eased.
I will take away her wickedness
and free her heart
so that she'll do right by God and
  by her husband
swearing off all malevolence."
345 Everyone wished her well,
that God should allow her soul
to benefit from her pure heart.
They made this heartfelt promise
  to her,
that they would not keep a lid on
  the news
350 but tell everyone about her.
The priests also said:
"We want to do the following:
whosoever is having his life
  ruined by his wife,
we will strongly suggest to him
355 that he bring her here
and have God bless him that
  way,
that she gain an understanding of
  what is good and right,
and also receive wisdom."
The news was spread
360 that the lady had been
the worst wife
who ever walked the earth
and was now the very best
woman known to be alive.

365 She had, furthermore, spread the
  word
that God had given her the power
to take away the evil
from every wicked wife that came
  to her.
Wherever the true story
370 of the enclosure was told,
in which the lady had been
  imprisoned
and what agony she suffered
  there—
torture that any woman might
  have to go through
if her husband bricked her in like
  that—
375 this tale made every wicked wife
  think:
"I would die
if they locked me up like that.
I will avoid getting myself in that
  kind of trouble.
I have decided to be good and
  pure, instead."
380 Every wife remembered that
  lesson
who lived in that land.
Both her sin and her shame
served as strong deterrents
so that their wickedness and their
  dishonor
385 simply vanished because of fear.
Nowhere in that land
could a wicked wife be found.
Through this most excellent tale
the lady became so highly
  regarded
390 that it was considered almost
  indecent

if someone had not met her face
   to face.
They called her the Holy Lady
and she became a site of
   pilgrimage.
Great praise and fame
395 followed her until death.

Many places today would be better
   off
if only they had someone
who would bring peace to men
from the actions of their wicked
   wives
who are evil, through and through.

Notes

Introduction

1. Freud, in his short essay "Medusa's Head," uses the Medusa myth to explain the castrating power of the malevolent female gaze. The terror of Medusa is the fear of castration linked to the sight of an uncanny object, such as the female sexual organ. Freud, *Sexuality and the Psychology of Love*, 212–13.

2. For a comprehensive discussion of this topic see Wade, *A Natural History of Vision*.

3. The intense gaze as an indicator of social relationships is applicable to all mammals. Staring is dominant and aggressive behavior, while looking down and avoiding the probing look of an opponent is understood as a sign of weakness and submission.

4. For related idioms see Schemann, *Deutsche Idiomatik*.

5. For further study of the evil-eye belief see Dundes, *The Evil Eye: A Folklore Casebook*.

6. A detailed anthropological examination of the almost universal evil-eye belief and the various preventative and curative measures taken is found in Maloney's *The Evil Eye*.

7. Burns discusses this elimination of women from the literary equation in *Bodytalk*, 13.

8. See Winnicott's "Mirror-Role of Mother and Family in Child Development" in *Playing and Reality*, 111–18.

Chapter 1. "A lady should never look directly at a male visitor": Thomasin von Zerclaere

1. The observations apply only to girls of noble descent. There are no records regarding the education of female peasants, due to the illiteracy of the peasant class and the clerical apathy toward them.

2. See Ehrismann 114–18 for a useful overview of the *huote* theme.

Chapter 2. "Wild glances": *Winsbeckin* and *Der Renner*

1. Rasmussen lists dating information, scholarly reception, extant manuscripts, and other codicological information regarding this text in *Mothers and Daughters*.

2. The maerkere and the watchdog theme is a trope in Minnesang. The secret lovers are always enraged against them. The female narrator of one of Meinloh von Sevelingen's songs curses the watchdogs, blaming them for the loss of her good reputation. "Sô wê den merkaeren! die habent mîn übele gedâht . . ." *Des Minnesangs Frühling*.

3. Detailed scholarly resources regarding this text can be found in Goheen's *Mensch und Moral im Mittelalter*.

4. Hugo shares *Der Renner*'s distaste of courtly pursuits; an English translation of the text *Von des todes gehugde* is found in the appendix of this volume. The title of the translation is "Remember Death."

5. For further study of this trope of medieval literature see Sinclair's *The Deceived Husband*.

Chapter 3. "The woman behind the wall": Heinrich von Melk and Der Stricker

1. The edition I use both for my discussion and the translation of the text, found in the appendix of this volume, is edited by Thomas Bein and Trude Ehlert, *Heinrich von Melk: Von des todes gehugde*.

2. See Ruh et al., *Die deutsche Literatur des Mittelalters*, vol. 5, col. 419.

3. See Schilling, *Der Stricker: Der Pfaffe Amis*.

4. My English translation is based on Ehrismann's Middle High German edition of Der Stricker's *Erzählungen, Fabeln, Reden*.

5. The religious aspects of immurement in the story are discussed in Wailes, "Immurement and Religious Experience."

6. For a detailed study of the tripartite socioeconomic structure, consult Duby's *The Three Orders: Feudal Society Imagined*.

Chapter 4. "He was as handsome as he could be!": Male Beauty and the Ogling Lady in the Eneasroman

1. In one of her earliest incarnations, Dido is a true classical heroine. After being widowed, she remains faithful to her murdered husband, committing suicide to avoid being taken by another man. Dido's noble character, however, is modified by the Roman historian Naevius, who connects her to the legend of Eneas and the foundation of Rome. His text recounts that Dido has a love affair with Eneas and kills herself after he abandons her. The better-known Dido character by Virgil is based on Naevius's version. For a concise account of the mythology surrounding Dido, see Grant's *Who's Who in Classical Mythology*. For a feminist reading of the character, see Desmond's *Reading Dido*.

2. A variation of this tale is found in the Norse epic *The Saga of the Volsungs*.

3. "Innan stokks" is the woman's domain of housework and child care and assumed to be inferior to the outside world of politics and power.

4. Curtius, in his *European Literature and the Latin Middle Ages*, argues that descriptions of requisite male beauty and of physical and moral excellence can be traced back to fixed schemata from Hellenistic times.

5. Thus, Dido becomes the predecessor of tragic heroines like Anna Karenina or Emma Bovary. They all lose their lives after giving in to their desires, while the men they idolized get away relatively unscathed.

6. Young girls loving knights by reputation alone is not an uncommon motif in European medieval literature. Guillaume de Machaut, in his fourteenth-century *Le livre du voir dit* has his female protagonist "burn with desire" to finally meet the narrator about whom she has heard so much. When she finally sees him, the much anticipated event proves anticlimactic; the love that had bubbled up between them—sight unseen—quickly evaporates.

7. Love entering through the eye is a classical concept that was widely accepted in the Middle Ages. André Le Chapelain, the medieval French cleric who wrote what is sometimes called the manual of courtly love, *De Amore*, informs us that love is born when seeing the beauty of someone of the opposite sex.

Chapter 5. "The most handsome knight that ever lived": Female Scopophilia in *Parzival*

1. The translations will be mine, unless otherwise noted.

2. Hatto, *Wolfram von Eschenbach: Parzival*, 73.

3. Müller, in his *Höfische Kompromisse*, shows how Arthur's court recognizes Parzival's innate nobility.

4. Bernheimer discusses the phallic symbolism of hands and fingers in figurative art in his article "The Uncanny Lure of Manet's Olympia," 13–27.

Chapter 6. "Lady, you saw it with your own eyes!": Enite and the Perfect Female Gaze in Hartmann's *Erec*

1. Guinevere is the best known among the Arthurian women. According to Fenster's argument in her introduction to *Arthurian Women*, Guinevere stands for a "zone of vulnerability in Arthur's realm." She is frequently associated with the theme of abduction.

2. For an excellent study of the metaphorical connection between silk and medieval noblewomen, see Burns's *Sea of Silk*.

3. Lacan, "L'amour courtois en anamorphose," in *Le séminaire: Livre VII*, 167–84.

4. For a thorough examination of the importance of dress in the Middle Ages see Burns's *Medieval Fabrications*.

5. The term *scopic economy* to describe the powers and pleasures of the gaze was coined by Caviness in *Visualizing Women in the Middle Ages*.

6. The term "prophet" is a translation of the participle of the verb "to see" in Hebrew, according to the *New Bible Dictionary*.

Chapter 7. Knight or Eye Candy? The Gendering Gaze in Hartmann
von Aue's *Iwein*

1. Never to judge a character by his or her outward appearance is a well-known motif in folktales and fairy tales. Young girls, old women, or even animals might be witches or fairies in disguise, wielding considerable magic powers. The Grimm's fairy tale "Frau Holle" is one example: an old crone is revealed to be a good fairy who rewards the industrious girl, while harshly punishing her lazy stepsister with a shower of molten tar.

2. Once again, the plot bears a resemblance to the narrative development in fairy tales. Most of the fairy-tale brides marry out of economic need (Cinderella) or out of thankfulness for being raised from a coma (Sleeping Beauty, Snow White). All of them live happily ever after, however vaguely that happiness is defined. Laudine's agreeing to a union with Iwein is based on similarly flimsy character and plot development.

3. Iwein is the knight who did too much, while Erec is the knight who did too little. Lancelot is the one who did just the right amount.

Bibliography

Allen, Peter. *The Art of Love: Amatory Fiction from Ovid to the Romance of the Rose.* Philadelphia: University of Pennsylvania Press, 1992.

Argyle, Michael. *Bodily Communication.* London: Methuen, 1975.

———. *Gaze and Mutual Gaze.* Cambridge: Cambridge University Press, 1976.

Aristotle. *De Partibus Animalium I and De Generatione Animalium I.* Trans. D. M. Balme. Oxford: Oxford University Press, 1992.

Arnold, Klaus. "Die Einstellung Zum Kind Im Mittelalter." *Mensch und Umwelt im Mittelalter.* Ed. Bernd Herrmann. Stuttgart: Deutsche Verlags-Anstalt, 1986. 53–64.

Ashley, Kathleen, et al. *Medieval Conduct.* Minneapolis: University of Minnesota Press, 2001.

Atkinson, Clarissa. *The Oldest Vocation: Christian Motherhood in the Middle Ages.* Ithaca: Cornell University Press, 1991.

Augustine. *Confessions.* Harmondsworth: Penguin, 1961.

Ayto, John. *Dictionary of Word Origins.* New York: Arcade, 1990.

Barthes, Roland. *Camera Lucida: Reflections on Photography.* London: Cape, 1982.

———. *Fragments d'un discours amoureux.* Paris: Éditions du Seuil, 1977.

Basil. *Ascetical Works.* Washington, DC: Catholic University of America Press, 1962.

Baswell, Christopher. "Men in the *Roman d'Eneas.* The Construction of Empire." *Medieval Masculinities: Regarding Men in the Middle Ages.* Ed. Clare Lees. Minneapolis: University of Minnesota Press, 1994. 149–68.

Bateson, Gregory. *Steps to an Ecology of Mind.* Chicago: University of Chicago Press, 2000.

Beauvoir, Simone de. *Le deuxième sexe.* Paris: Gallimard, 1976.

Bennett, Judith. *Ale, Beer, and Brewsters in England.* New York: Oxford University Press, 1996.

———. "Medievalism and Feminism." *Speculum* 68.2 (1993): 309–31.

———, ed. *Sisters and Workers in the Middle Ages.* Chicago: University of Chicago Press, 1989.

Benton, John F. "The Court of Champagne as a Literary Center." *Speculum* 36.4 (1961): 551–91.

Berger, John. *About Looking.* New York: Vintage Books, 1991.

———. *Ways of Seeing.* London: BBC and Penguin, 1972.

Bernheimer, Charles. "The Uncanny Lure of Manet's Olympia." *Seduction and Theory: Readings of Gender, Representation, and Rhetoric.* Ed. Dianne Hunter. Urbana: University of Illinois Press, 1989. 13–27.

Biddick, Kathleen. "Genders, Bodies, Borders: Technologies of the Visible." *Speculum* 68.2 (1993): 389–418.

Biernoff, Suzannah. *Sight and Embodiment in the Middle Ages.* New York: Palgrave MacMillan, 2002.

Blamires, Alcuin, ed. *Women Defamed and Women Defended.* Oxford: Oxford University Press, 1992.

Bloch, Howard. "Medieval Misogyny." *Representations* 20 (1986): 1–24.

———. *Medieval Misogyny and the Invention of Romantic Love.* Chicago: University of Chicago Press, 1991.

Bloch, Marc. *Feudal Society.* Andover: Routledge, 1989.

Bornstein, Diane. *The Lady in the Tower: Medieval Courtesy Literature for Women.* Hamden: Archon Books, 1983.

Bozovic, Miran. "The Man behind His Own Retina." *Everything You Always Wanted to Know about Lacan (But Were Afraid to Ask Hitchcock).* Ed. Slavoj Žižek. London: Verso, 1992. 161–77.

Brennan, Teresa. *Between Feminism and Psychoanalysis.* New York: Routledge, 1989.

Brinker-Von der Heyde, Claudia, and Ingrid Kasten. "Erziehung und Bildung in mittelalterlicher Literatur." *Der Deutschunterricht* 1.1 (2003): 3–4.

Bronfman, Judith. *"Chaucer's Clerk's Tale": The Griselda Story Received, Rewritten, Illustrated.* New York: Garland, 1994.

Brown, Joanne Carlson, and Carole Bohn, eds. *Christianity, Patriarchy, and Abuse: A Feminist Critique.* New York: Pilgrim Press, 1989.

Brundage, James. *Law, Sex, and Society in Medieval Europe.* Chicago: University of Chicago Press, 1987.

Bryson, Norman, and Michael Ann Holly. *Visual Culture: Images and Interpretations.* Hanover, NH: Wesleyan University Press of New England, 1994.

Bullough, Vern. "On Being a Male in the Middle Ages." *Medieval Masculinities: Regarding Men in the Middle Ages.* Ed. Claire Lees. Minneapolis: University of Minnesota Press, 1994. 31–45.

Bumke, Joachim. *Die Blutstropfen im Schnee: Über Wahrnehmung und Erkenntnis im "Parzival" Wolframs von Eschenbach.* Tübingen: Niemeyer, 2001.

———. *Geschichte der deutschen Literatur im Hohen Mittelalter.* München: Deutscher Taschenbuch Verlag, 1990.

———. "Geschlechterbeziehungen in den Gawan-Büchern von Wolframs Parzival." *Amsterdamer Beiträge zur älteren Germanistik* 38/39 (1994): 105–21.

———. *Höfische Kultur: Literatur und Gesellschaft im Hohen Mittelalter.* München: Deutscher Taschenbuch Verlag, 1999.

———. *Wolfram von Eschenbach.* Stuttgart: Metzler, 1991.

Burnett, Ron. *Cultures of Vision: Images, Media, and the Imaginary.* Bloomington: Indiana University Press, 1995.

Burns, E. Jane. *Bodytalk*. Philadelphia: University of Pennsylvania Press, 1993.

———, ed. *Medieval Fabrications: Dress, Textiles, Clothwork, and Other Cultural Imaginings*. New York: Palgrave Macmillan, 2004.

———. *Sea of Silk: A Textile Geography of Women's Work in Medieval French Literature*. Philadelphia: University of Pennsylvania Press, 2009.

———. "This Prick Which Is Not One: How Women Talk Back in Old French Fabliaux." *Feminist Approaches to the Body in Medieval Literature*. Ed. Linda Lomperis and Sarah Stanbury. Philadelphia: University of Pennsylvania Press, 1993. 188–212.

Burrow, John. *Gestures and Looks in Medieval Narrative*. Cambridge: Cambridge University Press, 2002.

Buschinger, Danielle, and Wolfgang Spiewok, eds. *Sex, Love, and Marriage in Medieval Literature and Reality*. Greifswald: Reineke Verlag, 1996.

Butler, Judith. *Bodies That Matter: On the Discursive Limits of Sex*. New York: Routledge, 1993.

———. *Gender Trouble: Feminism and the Subversion of Identity*. New York: Routledge, 1990.

Byars, Jackie. *All That Hollywood Allows: Re-Reading Gender in 1950s Melodrama*. Chapel Hill: University of North Carolina Press, 1991.

Bynum, Caroline Walker. *Jesus as Mother: Studies in the Spirituality of the High Middle Ages*. Berkeley: University of California Press, 1982.

Byock, Jesse L., ed. *The Saga of the Volsungs*. Berkeley: University of California Press, 1990.

Cadden, Joan. *Meanings of Sex Difference in the Middle Ages: Medicine, Science, and Culture*. Cambridge: Cambridge University Press, 1993.

Cantor, Norman. *Inventing the Middle Ages*. New York: William Morrow, 1991.

Carpenter, Jennifer, and Sally-Beth MacLean, eds. *Power of the Weak: Studies on Medieval Women*. Urbana: University of Illinois, 1995.

Cartlidge, Neil. *Medieval Marriage: Literary Approaches, 1100–1300*. Cambridge: D. S. Brewer, 1997.

Castelli, Elizabeth. "Virginity and Its Meaning for Women's Sexuality in Early Christianity." *Journal of Feminist Studies in Religion* 2 (1986): 61–88.

Caviness, Madeline. *Visualizing Women in the Middle Ages*. Philadelphia: University of Pennsylvania Press, 2001.

Cazelles, Brigitte. "Bodies on Stage and the Production of Meaning." *Yale French Studies* 86 (1994): 56–74.

———. *The Lady as Saint: A Collection of French Hagiographic Romances of the Thirteenth Century*. Philadelphia: University of Pennsylvania Press, 1991.

Chevalier, Jean, and Alain Gheerbrant. *A Dictionary of Symbols*. Cambridge, Mass: Blackwell, 1994.

Chodorow, Nancy. *Femininities, Masculinities, Sexualities*. Lexington: University Press of Kentucky, 1994.

———. *Feminism and Psychoanalytic Theory*. Cambridge, Mass.: Polity Press, 1989.

———. *The Power of Feeling*. New Haven: Yale University Press, 1999.

———. *Reproduction of Mothering: Psychoanalysis and the Sociology of Gender*. Berkeley: University of California Press, 1999.

Chrétien de Troyes. *Arthurian Romances*. Trans. William Kibler. London: Penguin, 1991.

———. *Erec and Enide*. Trans. Dorothy Gilbert. Berkeley: University of California Press, 1992.

———. *Perceval ou le Roman du Graal*. Paris: Gallimard, 1974.

Clark, Robert L. A. "Constructing the Female Subject in Late Medieval Devotion." *Medieval Conduct*. Ed. Kathleen Ashley and Robert L. A. Clark. Minneapolis: University of Minnesota Press, 2001. 160–82.

———. "Queering Gender and Naturalizing Class in the *Roman de Silence*." *Arthuriana* 12.1 (2002): 50–63.

Classen, Albrecht, ed. *Women as Protagonists in the German Middle Ages: An Anthology of Feminist Approaches to MHG Literature*. Göppingen: Kümmerle, 1991.

Clover, Carol. "Regardless of Sex: Men, Women, and Power in Early Northern Europe." *Speculum* 68.2 (1993): 363–87.

Cohen, Jeffrey, and Bonnie Wheeler, eds. *Becoming Male in the Middle Ages*. New York: Garland, 1997.

Coleman, Wil. "Doing Masculinity/Doing Theory." *Men, Masculinities and Social Theory*. Ed. Jeff Hearn and David Morgan. London: Unwin Hyman, 1990. 186–99.

Colledge, Edmund, and Bernard McGinn, eds. *Meister Eckhart: The Essential Sermons, Commentaries, Treatises and Defense*. New York: Paulist Press, 1981.

Cooey, Paula. *Religious Imagination and the Body: A Feminist Analysis*. Oxford: Oxford University Press, 1994.

Cooper, Brenda. "Chick Flicks as Feminist Texts: The Appropriation of the Male Gaze in Thelma and Louise." *Women's Studies in Communication* 23.3 (2000): 277–306.

Cox, Catherine. *Gender and Language in Chaucer*. Gainesville: University Press of Florida, 1997.

Cranny-Francis, Anne. *Engendered Fiction: Analysing Gender in the Production and Reception of Texts*. Kensington: University of South Wales Press, 1992.

Creed, Barbara. "Horror and the Monstrous Feminine: An Imaginary Abjection." *Screen* 27.1 (1986): 44–70.

Curtius, Ernst Robert. *European Literature and the Latin Middle Ages*. Princeton: Princeton University Press, 1990.

De Lauretis, Teresa. *Alice Doesn't: Feminism, Semiotics, Cinema*. Bloomington: Indiana University Press, 1984.

———. "Oedipus Interruptus." *Feminist Film Theory: A Reader*. Ed. Sue Thornham. New York: New York University Press, 1999. 83–96.

———. *Technologies of Gender*. Bloomington: Indiana University Press, 1987.

Delphy, Christine. "The Invention of French Feminism: An Essential Move." *Yale French Studies* 87 (1995): 190–221.

Denzin, Norman. *The Cinematic Society: The Voyeur's Gaze*. London: Sage, 1995.

Der Stricker. *Daniel von dem blühenden Tal*. Ed. Michael Resler. Tübingen: Max Niemeyer Verlag, 1995.

———. *Erzählungen, Fabeln, Reden.* Ed. Otfrid Ehrismann. Stuttgart: Reclam, 1992.

Desmond, Marilynn. *Reading Dido: Gender, Textuality, and the Medieval "Aeneid."* Minneapolis: University of Minnesota Press, 1994.

Dinzelbacher, Peter, ed. *Sachwörterbuch der Mediävistik.* Stuttgart: Kröner, 1992.

Doane, Mary Ann. "Caught and Rebecca: The Inscription of Femininity as Absence." *Feminist Film Theory: A Reader.* Ed. Sue Thornham. New York: New York University Press, 1999. 70–82.

———. *The Desire to Desire.* Bloomington: Indiana University Press, 1987.

———. *Femmes Fatales: Feminism, Film Theory, Psychoanalysis.* New York: Routledge, 1991.

———. "Film and the Masquerade: Theorising the Female Spectator." *Feminist Film Theory: A Reader.* Ed. Sue Thornham. New York: New York University Press, 1999. 131–45.

Dolar, Mladen. "A Father Who Is Not Quite Dead." *Everything You Always Wanted to Know about Lacan (But Were Afraid to Ask Hitchcock).* Ed. Slavoj Žižek. London: Verso, 1992. 143–50.

———. "Hitchcock's Objects." *Everything You Always Wanted to Know about Lacan (But Were Afraid to Ask Hitchcock).* Ed. Slavoj Žižek. London: Verso, 1992. 31–46.

———. "The Spectator Who Knew Too Much." *Everything You Always Wanted to Know about Lacan (But Were Afraid to Ask Hitchcock).* Ed. Slavoj Žižek. London: Verso, 1992. 129–36.

Douglas, J. D., ed. *New Bible Dictionary.* Wheaton: Tyndale House, 1982.

Dronzek, Anna. "Gendered Theories of Education in Fifteenth-Century Conduct Books." *Medieval Conduct.* Ed. Kathleen Ashley and Robert L. A. Clark. Minneapolis: University of Minnesota Press, 2001. 135–59.

Duby, Georges. *Love and Marriage in the Middle Ages.* Chicago: University of Chicago Press, 1994.

Dundes, Alan. *The Evil Eye: A Casebook.* New York: Garland, 1981.

———. *Oedipus: A Folklore Casebook.* New York: Garland, 1983.

———. *The Walled-Up Wife: A Casebook.* Madison: University of Wisconsin Press, 1996.

Dunton-Downer, Leslie. "Wolf Man." *Becoming Male in the Middle Ages.* Ed. Jeffrey Cohen and Bonnie Wheeler. New York: Garland, 2000. 203–18.

Eco, Umberto. *Interpretation and Overinterpretation.* Cambridge: Cambridge University Press, 1992.

Eggers, Hans. *Deutsche Sprachgeschichte: Das Althochdeutsche und das Mittelhochdeutsche.* Hamburg: Rowohlt, 1996.

Ehrismann, Otfried. *Ehre und Mut, Aventiure und Minne.* München: C. H. Beck, 1995.

Eigler, Friederike, and Susanne Kord, eds. *The Feminist Encyclopedia of German Literature.* Westport: Greenwood Press, 1997.

Ekman, Paul, ed. *Carl Darwin: The Expression of the Emotions in Man and Animal.* New York: Oxford University Press, 1998.

Elkins, James. *The Object Stares Back: On the Nature of Seeing.* New York: Simon & Schuster, 1996.

Eming, Jutta. "Subversion through Affirmation in the Stricker's *Eingemauerte Frau.*" *The Growth of Authority in the Medieval West.* Ed. Martin Gosman, Arjo Vanderjagt, and Jan Veestra. Groningen: Egbert Forsten, 1999. 213–28.

Erens, Patricia, ed. *Issues in Feminist Film Criticism.* Bloomington: Indiana University Press, 1990.

Fausto-Sterling, Anne. *Myths of Gender: Biological Theories About Women and Men.* New York: Basic Books, 1985.

———. *Sexing the Body: Gender Politics and the Construction of Sexuality.* New York: Basic Books, 2000.

Fenster, Thelma, ed. *Arthurian Women: A Casebook.* New York: Garland, 1996.

———. *Gender in Debate from the Early Middle Ages to the Renaissance.* New York: Palgrave, 2002.

Ferrante, Joan. *The Challenge of the Medieval Text: Studies in Genre and Interpretation.* New York: Columbia University Press, 1985.

———. "Cortes' Amor in Medieval Texts." *Speculum* 55.4 (1980): 686–95.

———. *To the Glory of Her Sex.* Bloomington: Indiana University Press, 1997.

———. *Woman as Image in Medieval Literature: From the Twelfth Century to Dante.* New York: Columbia University Press, 1975.

Fisher, Sheila, and Janet E. Hally, eds. *Seeking the Woman in Late Medieval and Renaissance Writing: Essays in Feminist Contextual Criticism.* Knoxville: University of Tennessee Press, 1989.

Fleischman, Suzanne. "Philology, Linguistics, and the Discourse of the Medieval Text." *Speculum* 65.1 (1990): 19–37.

Foster, Gwendolyn A. *Troping the Body: Gender, Etiquette, and Performance.* Carbondale: Southern Illinois University Press, 2000.

Fox, John Howard, ed. *Robert de Blois: Son oeuvre didactique et narrative.* Paris: Librairie Nizet, 1950.

Frakes, Jerold. *Brides and Doom: Gender, Property, and Power in Medieval German Women's Epic.* Philadelphia: University of Pennsylvania Press, 1994.

Frantzen, Allen. "When Women Aren't Enough." *Speculum* 68.2 (1993): 445–71.

Freidank. *Bescheidenheit.* Ed. Wolfgang Spiewok. Leipzig: Reclam, 1991.

Frenzel, Elisabeth. *Stoffe der Weltliteratur.* Stuttgart: Kröner, 1998.

Freud, Sigmund. *Drei Abhandlungen zur Sexualtheorie.* Frankfurt am Main: Fischer Verlag, 2002.

———. *Sexuality and the Psychology of Love.* New York: Collier, 1963.

———. *Totem und Tabu.* Frankfurt am Main: Fischer Verlag, 1940.

———. *Die Traumdeutung.* Frankfurt am Main: Fischer Verlag, 2002.

———. *Das Unbewusste: Schriften zur Psychoanalyse.* Frankfurt am Main: Fischer Verlag, 1964.

Freud, Sigmund, and Joseph Breuer. *Studien über Hysterie.* Frankfurt am Main: Fischer Verlag, 2000.

Fries, Maureen. "Female Heroes, Heroines, and Counter-Heroes." *Arthurian Women.* Ed. Thelma Fenster. New York: Routledge, 1996. 59–73.

Fuhrmann, Horst. *Germany in the High Middle Ages ca. 1050–1200*. New York: Cambridge University Press, 1986.

Gallop, Jane. *The Daughter's Seduction: Feminism and Psychoanalysis*. Ithaca: Cornell University Press, 1982.

Gamman, Lorraine, and Margaret Marshment, eds. *The Female Gaze: Women as Viewers of Popular Culture*. London: Women's Press, 1987.

Gaunt, Simon. *Gender and Genre in Medieval French Literature*. Cambridge: Cambridge University Press, 1995.

Genzmer, Felix, ed. *Das Nibelungenlied*. Stuttgart: Reclam, 1997.

Gerritsen, Willem Peter, et al. *A Dictionary of Medieval Heroes: Characters in Medieval Narrative Traditions and their Afterlife in Literature, Theatre, and the Visual Arts*. Rochester: Boydell Press, 1998.

Geyer, Felix, and Johannes van der Zouwen. "Cybernetics and Social Science: Theories and Research in Sociocybernetics." *Kybernetes* 20.6 (1991): 81–92.

Gibbs, Marion, and Sidney Johnson. *Medieval German Literature*. New York: Garland, 1997.

Gies, Frances. *The Knight in History*. New York: Harper and Row, 1984.

Goddard, Kevin. "Look Maketh the Man: The Female Gaze and the Construction of Masculinity." *Journal of Men's Studies* 9.1 (2000): 23–39.

Goheen, Jutta. *Mensch und Moral im Mittelalter: Geschichte und Fiktion in Hugo von Trimbergs Der Renner*. Darmstadt: Wissenschaftliche Buchgesellschaft, 1990.

Gottfried von Strassburg. *Tristan*. Ed. Friedrich Ranke. Stuttgart: Reclam, 1998.

Grant, Michael. *Who's Who in Classical Mythology*. Oxford: Oxford University Press, 1993.

Gravdal, Kathryn. *Ravishing Maidens: Writing Rape in Medieval French Literature and Law*. Philadelphia: University of Pennsylvania Press, 1991.

Green, Monica. "Female Sexuality in the Medieval West." *Trends in History* 4 (1990): 127–58.

Grimm, Gunter, and Frank Max, eds. *Deutsche Dichter*. Vol. 1 of *Mittelalter*. Stuttgart: Reclam, 1994.

Grimm, Jacob, and Willhelm Grimm. *Grimms Märchen: Eine Auslese*. Ljubljana: Manfred Pawlak Verlag, 1989.

Gurevich, Aron. *Medieval Popular Culture: Problems of Belief and Perception*. New York: Cambridge University Press, 1990.

Haaken, Janice. "Bitch and Femme Psychology: Women, Aggression, and Psychoanalytic Social Theory." *Journal for the Psychoanalysis of Culture and Society* 7.2 (2002): 202–25.

Hamilton, Victoria. *Narcissus and Oedipus: The Children of Psychoanalysis*. London: Karnac Books, 1993.

Hartmann von Aue. *Der arme Heinrich*. Ed. Ursula Rautenberg. Trans. Siegfried Grosse. Stuttgart: Reclam, 1999.

———. *Erec*. Ed. Thomas Cramer. Frankfurt am Main: Fischer Verlag, 1998.

———. *Iwein*. Ed. Thomas Cramer. Berlin: de Gruyter, 1974.

Haskell, Molly. "The Woman's Film." *Feminist Film Theory: A Reader*. Ed. Sue Thornham. New York: New York University Press, 1999. 20–30.

Hasty, Will. *Adventures in Interpretation: The Works of Hartmann von Aue and Their Critical Reception*. Columbia, SC: Camden House, 1996.

———. *A Companion to Gottfried von Strassburg's "Tristan."* Columbia, S.C.: Camden House, 2003.

Hatto, Arthur Thomas. *Wolfram von Eschenbach: Parzival*. London: Penguin, 1980.

Hearn, Jeff, and David Morgan, eds. *Men, Masculinities and Social Theory*. London: Unwin Hyman, 1990.

Heinrich von Melk. *Von des Todes Gehugde: Mahnrede über den Tod*. Ed. Thomas Bein and Trude Ehlert. Stuttgart: Reclam, 1994.

Heinrich von Veldeke. *Eneasroman*. Trans. Ludwig Ettmüller. Ed. Dieter Kartschoke. Stuttgart: Reclam, 1986.

Hennig, Beate. *Kleines Mittelhochdeutsches Wörterbuch*. Tübingen: Max Niemeyer Verlag, 1998.

Heyworth, Gregory. *Desiring Bodies: Ovidian Romance and the Cult of Form*. Notre Dame: University of Notre Dame Press, 2009.

Hinde, Robert, ed. *Non-Verbal Communication*. Cambridge: Cambridge University Press, 1972.

Hoffman, Donald. "Perceval's Sister: Malory's 'Rejected' Masculinities." *Arthuriana* 6.4 (1996): 72–83.

Horowitz, Maryanne Cline. "Aristotle and Women." *Journal of the History of Biology* 9.2 (1976): 183–213.

Hugo von Trimberg. *Der Renner*. Ed. Gustav Ehrismann. Berlin: de Gruyter, 1970.

Humm, Maggie. *Feminism and Film*. Bloomington: Indiana University Press, 1997.

Hunter, Dianne, ed. *Seduction and Theory*. Urbana: University of Illinois Press, 1989.

Irigaray, Luce. *Speculum of the Other Woman*. Ithaca: Cornell University Press, 1985.

———. *This Sex Which Is Not One*. Ithaca: Cornell University Press, 1985.

Isidor of Seville. *Etymologiae*. Oxford: Oxford University Press, 1962.

Jackson, William. *Chivalry in Twelfth-Century Germany: The Works of Hartmann von Aue*. Cambridge, MA: D. S. Brewer, 1994.

Jaeger, Stephen. *Ennobling Love: In Search of a Lost Sensibility*. Philadelphia: University of Pennsylvania Press, 1999.

Jochens, Jenny. "The Medieval Icelandic Heroine: Fact or Fiction?" *Viator* 19 (1986): 35–50.

Johnston, Claire. *Notes on Women's Cinema*. London: Society for Education in Film and Television, 1973.

———. "Women's Cinema as Counter-Cinema." *Feminist Film Theory: A Reader*. Ed. Sue Thornham. New York: New York University Press, 1999. 31–40.

Johnston, Mark, ed. *Medieval Conduct Literature*. Toronto: University of Toronto Press, 2009.

Kaplan, E. Ann, ed. *Feminism and Film*. Oxford: Oxford University Press, 2000.

———. "Is the Gaze Male?" *Feminism and Film*. Ed. E. Ann Kaplan. Oxford: Oxford University Press, 2000. 119–38.

———. *Psychoanalysis and Cinema*. London: Routledge, 1990.

Kartschoke, Dieter. *Geschichte der deutschen Literatur im Frühen Mittelalter*. München: Deutscher Taschenbuch Verlag, 2000.

———. "Heinrich von Veldecke." *Deutsche Dichter*. Vol. 1 of *Mittelalter*. Ed. Gunter Grimm and Frank Max. Stuttgart: Reclam, 1994. 132–41.

Kasten, Ingrid, ed. *Frauenlieder des Mittelalters*. Stuttgart: Reclam, 1990.

———. "Häßliche Frauenfiguren in der Literatur des Mittelalters." *Auf der Suche nach der Frau im Mittelalter*. Ed. Bea Lundt. München: Fink, 1991. 255–76.

———. "Herrschaft und Liebe: Zur Rolle und Darstellung des Helden im *Roman d' Eneas* und in Veldekes *Eneasroman*." *Deutsche Vierteljahrsschrift für Literaturwissenschaft und Geistesgeschichte* 62 (1988): 227–45.

Kates, Gary. "The Transgendered World of the Chevalier/Chevalière d'Eon." *Journal of Modern History* 67.3 (1995): 558–94.

Kelly, Douglas. *Medieval French Romance*. New York: Twayne, 1993.

Kelly, Kathleen Coyne. "Malory's Body Chivalric." *Arthuriana* 6.4 (1996): 52–71.

Kennedy, Edward, ed. *King Arthur: A Casebook*. New York: Garland, 1996.

Kimmel, Michael. *The Gendered Society*. New York: Oxford University Press, 2000.

Knapp, Mark. *Non-Verbal Communication in Human Interaction*. London: Wadsworth, 2001.

Kofman, Sarah. *The Enigma of Woman*. Ithaca: Cornell University Press, 1985.

Kohlschmidt, Werner, and Wolfgang Mohr, eds. *Reallexikon der deutschen Literaturgeschichte*. 5 vols. Berlin: de Gruyter, 1958.

Kristeva, Julia. *Powers of Horror: An Essay on Abjection*. New York: Columbia University Press, 1982.

Kritzman, Lawrence. "Roland Barthes: The Discourse of Desire and the Question of Gender." *Modern Language Notes* 103.4 (1988): 848–64.

Krohn, Rüdiger. "Gottfried von Straßburg." *Deutsche Dichter*. Vol. 1 of *Mittelalter*. Ed. Gunter Grimm and Frank Max. Stuttgart: Reclam, 1994. 217–35.

Krueger, Roberta. *The Cambridge Companion to Medieval Romance*. Cambridge: Cambridge University Press, 2000.

———. "Constructing Sexual Identities in the High Middle Ages: The Didactic Poetry of Robert de Blois." *Paragraph* 13 (1990). 105–31.

———. "Love, Honor, and the Exchange of Women in Yvain." *Arthurian Women*. Ed. Thelma Fenster. New York: Routledge, 1996. 3–18.

———. "Nouvelles Choses." *Medieval Conduct*. Ed. Kathleen Ashley and Robert L. A. Clark. Minneapolis: University of Minnesota Press, 2001. 49–85.

Kruse, Britta-Juliane. "Women's Secrets." *Sex, Love and Marriage in Medieval Literature and Reality*. Ed. Danielle Buschinger and Wolfgang Spiewok. Greifswald: Reineke Verlag, 1996. 33–40.

Kudrun. Ed. Bernhard Sowinski. Stuttgart: Reclam, 1995.

Lacan, Jacques. *The Four Fundamental Concepts of Psychoanalysis*. New York: Norton, 1998.

———. *Le séminaire: Livre VII: L'éthique de la psychanalyse 1959–60*. Paris: Éditions du Seuil, 1986.

Lacy, Norris. "Sex and Love in the Fabliaux." *Sex, Love and Marriage in Medieval Literature and Reality*. Ed. Danielle Buschinger and Wolfgang Spiewok. Greifswald: Reineke-Verlag, 1996. 41–46.

Laqueur, Thomas. *Making Sex: Body and Gender from the Greeks to Freud*. Cambridge: Harvard University Press, 1990.

Le Chapelain, André. *Traité de l'amour courtois*. Paris: Klincksieck, 1974.

Lees, Clare. "Men and Beowulf." *Medieval Masculinities: Regarding Men in the Middle Ages*. Ed. Clare Lees. Minneapolis: University of Minnesota Press, 1994. 129–48.

———. *Tradition and Belief: Religious Writing in Late Anglo-Saxon England*. Minneapolis: University of Minnesota Press, 1999.

———, ed. *Medieval Masculinities: Regarding Men in the Middle Ages*. Minneapolis: University of Minnesota Press, 1994.

Lehman, Peter. *Running Scared: Masculinity and the Representation of the Male Body*. Philadelphia: Temple University Press, 1993.

Leitzmann, Albert, ed. *Winsbeckische Gedichte nebst Tirol und Fridebrand*. Tübingen: Niemeyer, 1962.

Lévi-Strauss, Claude. *The Elementary Structures of Kinship*. Boston: Beacon Press, 1969.

Lewis, Clide Staples. *The Allegory of Love: A Study in Mediaeval Tradition*. Oxford: Oxford University Press, 1951.

Lienert, Elisabeth. *Deutsche Antikenromane des Mittelalters*. Berlin: Erich Schmidt, 2001.

Lomperis, Linda, and Sarah Stanbury, eds. *Feminist Approaches to the Body in Medieval Literature*. Philadelphia: University of Pennsylvania Press, 1993.

Lundt, Bea, ed. *Auf der Suche nach der Frau im Mittelalter*. München: Fink, 1991.

MacCormack, Carol, and Marylin Strathern, eds. *Nature, Culture, and Gender*. New York: Cambridge University Press, 1980.

Machaut, Guillaume de. *Le livre du voir dit*. Ed. Paul Imbs. Paris: Librairie Générale Française, 1999.

Maloney, Clarence, ed. *The Evil Eye*. New York: Columbia University Press, 1976.

Marshall, Cynthia. "Psychoanalyzing the Prepsychoanalytic Subject." *PMLA* 117 (2002): 1207–16.

Mayne, Judith. *Cinema and Spectatorship*. London: Routledge, 1993.

McCallum, Ellen Lee. *Object Lessons: How to Do Things with Fetishism*. Albany: State University of New York Press, 1999.

McCracken, Peggy. "The Body Politic and the Queen's Adulterous Body in French Romance." *Feminist Approaches to the Body in Medieval Literature*. Ed. Linda Lomperis and Sarah Stanbury. Philadelphia: University of Pennsylvania Press, 1993. 38–64.

McMahon, James V. "Enite's Relatives: The Girl in the Garden." *Modern Language Notes* 85.3 (1970): 367–72.

McNamara, Jo Ann. "The 'Herrenfrage.' The Restructuring of the Gender System, 1050–1150." *Medieval Masculinities: Regarding Men in the Middle Ages.* Ed. Clare Lees. Minneapolis: University of Minnesota Press, 1994. 3–29.

Menge, Hermann. *Taschenwörterbuch der lateinischen und deutschen Sprache.* Berlin: Langenscheidt, 1963.

Mertens, Volker. "Hartmann von Aue." *Deutsche Dichter.* Vol. 1 of *Mittelalter.* Ed. Gunter Grimm and Frank Max. Stuttgart: Reclam, 1994. 164–79.

———. *Laudine: Soziale Problematik im Iwein Hartmanns von Aue.* Berlin: Erich Schmidt, 1978.

Mertens, Volker, and Ulrich Müller. *Epische Stoffe des Mittelalters.* Stuttgart: Kröner, 1984.

Metz, Christian. "The Imaginary Signifier." *Screen* 16.2 (1975).

Mitchell, Juliet. *Psychoanalysis and Feminism: A Radical Reassessment of Freudian Psychoanalysis.* New York: Basic Books, 2000.

Modleski, Tania. *Loving with a Vengeance: Mass-Produced Fantasies for Women.* Hamden: Archon Books, 1982.

———. *Old Wives' Tales, and Other Women's Stories.* New York: New York University Press, 1998.

———. *The Terror of Pleasure: The Contemporary Horror Film and Postmodern Theory.* Milwaukee: University of Wisconsin Press, 1984.

———. *The Women Who Knew Too Much.* New York: Methuen, 1988.

Moi, Toril, ed. *The Kristeva Reader.* New York: Columbia University Press, 1986.

———. *Sexual Textual Politics.* New York: Routledge, 1995.

———. *What Is a Woman?* Oxford: Oxford University Press, 2001.

Monson, Don. "Andreas Capellanus and the Problem of Irony." *Speculum* 63.3 (1988): 539–72.

———. "The Troubadour's Lady Reconsidered Again." *Speculum* 70.2 (1995): 255–74.

Montrose, Louis. "The Work of Gender in the Discourse of Discovery." *Representations* 33 (1991): 1–41.

Morawski, Jill. *Practicing Feminisms, Reconstructing Psychology.* Ann Arbor: University of Michigan Press, 1994.

Morrow, Collette. "'To See and to Know . . . ': Female Gazing in Julian of Norwich's 'Showings.'" *Magistra: A Journal of Women's Spirituality in History* 3.1 (1997): 3–31.

Moser, Hugo, and Helmut Tervooren, eds. *Des Minnesangs Frühling.* 38th ed. Stuttgart: Hirzel Verlag, 1988.

Müller, Jan-Dirk. *Höfische Kompromisse: Acht Kapitel zur höfischen Epik.* Tübingen: Max Niemeyer, 2007.

Mulvey, Laura. *Visual and Other Pleasures.* Bloomington: Indiana University Press, 1989.

Murray, Jacqueline, ed. *Conflicted Identities and Multiple Masculinities: Men in the Medieval West.* New York: Garland, 1999.

Nellmann, Eberhard. *Wolframs Erzähltechnik: Untersuchungen zur Funktion des Erzählers.* Wiesbaden: Steiner, 1973.

Newman, Barbara. "Authority, Authenticity, and the Repression of Heloise." *Journal of Medieval and Renaissance Studies* 22.2 (1992): 121–57.

———. *From Virile Woman to Womanchrist: Studies in Medieval Religion and Literature.* Philadelphia: University of Pennsylvania Press, 1995.

Newman, Jane O. "Sons and Mothers: Agrippina, Semiramis, and the Philological Construction of Gender Roles in Early Modern Germany." *Renaissance Quarterly* 49.1 (1996): 77–113.

Nissé, Ruth. "Grace under Pressure: Conduct and Representation in the Norwich Heresy Trials." *Medieval Conduct.* Ed. Kathleen Ashley and Robert L. A. Clark. Minneapolis: University of Minnesota Press, 2001. 207–25.

Nusser, Peter. *Deutsche Literatur im Mittelalter.* Stuttgart: Kröner, 1992.

Ovid. *The Metamorphoses.* New York: Viking Press, 1958.

Patterson, Lee. "Chaucer's Pardoner on the Couch: Psyche and Clio in Medieval Literary Studies." *Speculum* 76 (2001): 638–80.

———. *Negotiating the Past.* Madison: University of Wisconsin Press, 1987.

Paxon, James. *Desiring Discourse: The Literature of Love, Ovid through Chaucer.* Selinsgrove: Susquehanna University Press, 1998.

Perfetti, Lisa, ed. *The Representation of Women's Emotions in Medieval and Early Modern Culture.* Gainesville: University Press of Florida, 2005.

Plummer, John F. "Frenzy and Females." *Arthuriana* 6.4 (1996): 45–51.

Power, Eileen. *Medieval Women.* Cambridge: Cambridge University Press, 1995.

Pribam, E. Deidre, ed. *Female Spectators: Looking at Film and Television.* New York: Verso, 1988.

Ramey, Lynn. "Representation of Women in Chrétien's 'Erec et Enide': Courtly Literature or Misogyny?" *Romantic Review* 84.4 (1993): 377–86.

Rasmussen, Ann Marie. "Fathers to Think Back Through." *Medieval Conduct.* Ed. Kathleen Ashley and Robert L. A. Clark. Minneapolis: University of Minnesota Press, 2001. 106–34.

———. "The Female Figures in Gottfried's *Tristan and Isolde.*" *A Companion to Gottfried von Strassburg's "Tristan."* Ed. Will Hasty. Columbia: Camden House, 2003. 137–57.

———. "Gendered Knowledge and Eavesdropping in the Late-Medieval Minnerede." *Speculum* 77 (2002): 1168–94.

———. "Medieval German Romance." *Medieval Romance.* Ed. Roberta Krueger. Cambridge: Cambridge University Press, 2000. 183–202.

———, ed. *Medieval Woman's Song: Cross-Cultural Approaches.* Philadelphia: University of Pennsylvania Press, 2002.

———. *Mothers and Daughters in Medieval German Literature.* New York: Syracuse University Press, 1997.

Reiter, Raina. *Of Woman Born.* New York: Norton, 1995.

———, ed. *Toward an Anthropology of Women.* New York: Monthly Review Press, 1975.

Rich, B. Ruby. "The Crisis of Naming in Feminist Film Criticism." *Feminist Film Theory: A Reader.* Ed. Sue Thornham. New York: New York University Press, 1999. 41–49.

Riddy, Felicity. "Mother Knows Best: Reading Social Change in a Courtesy Text." *Speculum* 71.1 (1996): 66–86.

Roberts, Anna, ed. *Violence against Women in Medieval Texts*. Gainesville: University Press of Florida, 1998.

Röcke, Werner. "Lehrdichtung." *Deutsche Dichter*. Vol. 1 of *Mittelalter*. Ed. Gunter Grimm and Frank Max. Stuttgart: Reclam, 1994. 442–57.

Rodowick, David. *The Difficulty of Difference*. New York: Routledge, 1991.

Roper, Lyndal. *Oedipus and the Devil: Witchcraft, Sexuality and Religion in Early Modern Europe*. London: Routledge, 1994.

Rose, Jacqueline. *Sexuality in the Field of Vision*. London: Verso, 1986.

Rubin, Gayle. "The Traffic in Women: Notes on the 'Political Economy of Sex.'" *Toward an Anthropology of Women*. Ed. Raina Reiter. New York: Monthly Review Press, 1975. 157–210.

Rückle, Horst. *Körpersprache verstehen und deuten*. Wiesbaden: Falken-Verlag, 1991.

Ruh, Kurt, et al., eds. *Die deutsche Literatur des Mittelalters—Verfasserlexikon*. 5 vols. Berlin: de Gruyter, 1980.

Russ, Anja. *Kindheit und Adoleszenz in den deutschen Parzival—und Lanzelotromanen*. Stuttgart: Hirzel, 2000.

Salecl, Renata, and Slavoj Žižek. *Gaze and Voice as Love Objects*. Durham: Duke University Press, 1996.

Salisbury, Eve. *Domestic Violence in Medieval Texts*. Gainesville: University Press of Florida, 2002.

Salisbury, Joyce, ed. *Sex in the Middle Ages: A Book of Essays*. New York: Garland, 1991.

Scala, Elizabeth. "Historicists and Their Discontents: Reading Psychoanalytically in Medieval Studies." *Texas Studies in Literature and Language* 44.1 (2002): 108–31.

Scheman, Naomi. "Missing Mothers/Desiring Daughters: Framing the Sight of Women." *Critical Inquiry* 15 (1988): 62–89.

Schilling, Michael. "Der Stricker." *Deutsche Dichter*. Vol. 1 of *Mittelalter*. Ed. Gunter Grimm and Frank Max. Stuttgart: Reclam, 1994. 297–310.

Schröder, Werner. *Irrungen und Wirrungen um den Text von Hartmanns "Erec."* Stuttgart: F. Steiner, 1996.

———. "Wolfram von Eschenbach." *Deutsche Dichter*. Vol. 1 of *Mittelalter*. Ed. Gunter Grimm and Frank Max. Stuttgart: Reclam, 1994. 180–216.

Schroeder, Jonathan. "Consuming Representation: A Visual Approach to Consumer Research." *Representing Consumers: Voices, Views and Visions*. Ed. Barbara Stern. London: Routledge, 1998. 193–230.

Schultz, James A. "Bodies That Don't Matter: Heterosexuality Before Heterosexuality in Gottfried's Tristan." *Constructing Medieval Sexuality*. Ed. Karma Lochrie, Peggy McCracken and James A. Schultz. Minneapolis: University of Minnesota Press, 1997. 91–110.

———. "Classical Rhetoric, Medieval Poetics, and the Medieval Vernacular Prologue." *Speculum* 59 (1984): 1–15.

————. "Medieval Adolescence: The Claims of History and the Silence of German Narrative." *Speculum* 66 (1991): 519–39.

————. *The Shape of the Round Table: Structures of Middle High German Arthurian Romance.* Toronto: University of Toronto Press, 1983.

Schulze-Belli, Paola. *Liebe und Aventiure im Artusroman des Mittelalters.* Göppingen: Kümmerle, 1990.

Schwartz, Regina. "Rethinking Voyeurism and Patriarchy: The Case of Paradise Lost." *Representations* 34 (1991): 85–103.

Sedgwick, Eve. *Between Men: English Literature and Homosocial Desire.* New York: Columbia University Press, 1985.

Semple, Benjamin. "The Male Psyche and the Female Sacred Body in Marie de France and Christine de Pizan." *Yale French Studies* 86 (1994): 164–86.

Showalter, Elaine, ed. *Speaking of Gender.* New York: Routledge, 1989.

Siebers, Tobin. *The Mirror of Medusa.* Berkeley: University of California Press, 1983.

Sigal, Gale. *Erotic Dawn Songs of the Middle Ages: Voicing the Lyric Lady.* Gainesville: University Press of Florida, 1996.

Silverman, Kaja. *The Acoustic Mirror: The Female Voice in Psychoanalysis and Cinema.* Bloomington: Indiana University Press, 1988.

————. "Lost Objects and Mistaken Subjects." *Feminist Film Theory: A Reader.* Ed. Sue Thornham. New York: New York University Press, 1999. 97–107.

————. *Male Subjectivity at the Margins.* London: Routledge, 1992.

————. "What Is a Camera? or: History in the Field of Vision." *Discourse* 15.3 (1993): 3–56.

Simmons, Clare. *Medievalism and the Quest for the "Real" Middle Ages.* London: F. Cass, 2001.

Sinclair, Alison. *The Deceived Husband: A Kleinian Approach to the Literature of Infidelity.* Oxford: Clarendon Press, 1993.

Smith, Sharon. "The Image of Women in Film: Some Suggestions For Future Research." *Feminist Film Theory: A Reader.* Ed. Sue Thornham. New York: New York University Press, 1999. 14–19.

Sobchack, Vivian. *The Address of the Eye: A Phenomenology of Film Experience.* Princeton: Princeton University Press, 1992.

Solterer, Helen. *The Master and Minerva.* Berkeley: University of California Press, 1995.

Spence, Sarah. "'Lo Cop Mortal': The Evil Eye and the Origins of Courtly Love." *Romantic Review* 87.3 (1996): 307–23.

Squier, Susan. "Mirroring and Mothering: Reflections on the Mirror Encounter Metaphor in Virginia Woolf's Works." *Twentieth Century Literature* 27.3 (1981): 272–88.

Stanbury, Sarah. "Feminist Masterplots: The Gaze on the Body of Pearl's Dead Girl." *Feminist Approaches to the Body in Medieval Literature.* Ed. Linda Lomperis and Sarah Stanbury. Philadelphia: University of Pennsylvania Press, 1993. 96–115.

————. *Seeing the Gawain-Poet: Description and the Act of Perception.* Philadelphia: University of Pennsylvania Press, 1991.

———. "The Virgin's Gaze: Spectacle and Transgression in Middle English Lyrics of the Passion." *PMLA* 106 (1991): 1083–93.

Steiner, Arpad. *De Eruditione Filiorum Nobilium of Vincent of Beauvais*. Cambridge: Cambridge University Press, 1939.

Sterba, Wendy. "The Question of Enite's Transgression: Female Voice and Male Gaze as Determining Factors in Hartmann's Erec." *Women as Protagonists in the German Middle Ages: An Anthology of Feminist Approaches to MHG Literature*. Ed. Albrecht Classen. Göppingen: Kümmerle, 1991. 57–68.

Sterling-Hellenbrand, Alexandra. *Topographies of Gender in Middle High German Arthurian Romance*. New York: Garland, 2001.

Strohm, Paul. *Theory and the Premodern Text*. Minneapolis: University of Minnesota Press, 2000.

Studlar, Gaylyn. *In the Realm of Pleasure: Von Sternberg, Dietrich, and the Masochistic Aesthetic*. New York: Columbia University Press, 1988.

Synnott, Anthony. "A Sociology of Smell." *Canadian Review of Sociology and Anthropology* 28.4 (1991): 437–60.

Taylor, Karen, ed. *Gender Transgressions: Grossing the Normative Barrier in Old French Literature*. New York: Garland, 1998.

Theweleit, Klaus. *Male Fantasies*. Minneapolis: University of Minnesota Press, 1987.

Thornham, Sue, ed. *Feminist Film Theory: A Reader*. New York: New York University Press, 1999.

van Rinsum, Annemarie, and Wolfgang van Rinsum. *Lexikon literarischer Gestalten*. Stuttgart: Kröner, 1988.

Volfing, Annette. "Gottfried's Huote Excursus." *Medium Aevum* 67.1 (1998): 85–108.

Wack, Mary Frances. *Lovesickness in the Middle Ages*. Philadelphia: University of Pennsylvania Press, 1990.

Wade, Nicolas. *A Natural History of Vision*. Cambridge: MIT Press, 1999.

Wahrig, Gerhard. *Wörterbuch der deutschen Sprache*. München: DTV, 1978.

Wailes, Stephen. "Immurement and Religious Experience in the Stricker's *Eingemauerte Frau*." *Beiträge zur Geschichte der deutschen Sprache und Literatur* 96 (1974): 79–102.

———. *Studien zur Kleindichtung des Strickers*. Berlin: Erich Schmidt, 1981.

Walker Bynum, Caroline. "Fast, Feast, and Flesh: The Religious Significance of Food to Medieval Women." *Representations* 11 (1985): 1–25.

———. *Holy Feast and Holy Fast: The Religious Significance of Food to Medieval Women*. Berkeley: University of California Press, 1987.

———. *The Resurrection of the Body in Western Christianity*. New York: Columbia University Press, 1995.

Watt, Diane. *Medieval Women in Their Communities*. Cardiff: University of Wales Press, 1997.

Weddige, Hilkert. *Einführung in die germanistische Mediävistik*. München: C. H. Beck, 1997.

———. *Mittelhochdeutsch*. München: C. H. Beck, 1998.

Wehrli, Max. *Literatur im deutschen Mittelalter*. Stuttgart: Reclam, 1998.

Wendell, Vernon Clausen. *Virgil's "Aeneid" and the Tradition of Hellenistic Poetry*. Berkeley: University of California Press, 1987.

Wenzel, Horst. *Hören und Sehen, Schrift und Bild: Kultur und Gedächtnis im Mittelalter*. München: C. H. Beck, 1995.

———. "Öffentlichkeit und Heimlichkeit in Gottfried's 'Tristan.'" *Zeitschrift für deutsche Philologie* 107 (1988): 335–61.

Wernher der Gartenaere. *Helmbrecht*. Ed. Friedrich Panzer and Kurt Roh. Tübingen: Max Niemeyer, 1993.

Westphal, Sarah. "Bad Girls in the Middle Ages: Gender, Law, and German Literature." *Essays in Medieval Studies* 19 (2002): 103–19.

———. "Camilla: The Amazon Body in Medieval German Literature." *Exemplaria* 8.1 (1996): 231–58.

———. *Textual Poetics of German Manuscripts 1300–1500*. Columbia, S.C.: Camden House, 1993.

Westphal-Wihl, Sarah. "The Ladies' Tournament: Marriage, Sex, and Honor in Thirteenth-Century Germany." *Sisters and Workers in the Middle Ages*. Ed. Judith Bennett and Elizabeth Clark. Chicago: University of Chicago Press, 1989. 162–89.

Wetzlmair, Wolfgang. *Zum Problem der Schuld im "Erec" und im "Gregorius" Hartmanns von Aue*. Göppingen: Kümmerle, 1997.

Wilk, Stephen. *Medusa: Solving the Mystery of the Gorgon*. Oxford: Oxford University Press, 2000.

Wilkinson, Sue, and Celia Kitzinger, eds. *Feminism and Discourse*. London: Sage Publications, 1995.

Willms, Eva, ed. *Thomasin von Zerklaere: Der Welsche Gast*. Berlin: de Gruyter, 2004.

Wilson, Katharina. *Wykked Wyves and the Woes of Marriage: Misogamous Literature from Juvenal to Chaucer*. Albany: SUNY Press, 1990.

Winnicott, Donald. *Playing and Reality*. New York: Routledge, 2001.

Wolfram von Eschenbach. *Parzival*. Trans. and ed. Karl Lachmann. Stuttgart: Reclam, 1997.

Wolterbeek, Marc. *Comic Tales of the Middle Ages: An Anthology and Commentary*. New York: Greenwood Press, 1991.

Žižek, Slavoj, ed. *Everything You Always Wanted to Know about Lacan (But Were Afraid to Ask Hitchcock)*. London: Verso, 1992.

———. *The Fragile Absolute*. London: Verso, 2000.

———. "Hitchcockian Sinthoms." *Everything You Always Wanted to Know about Lacan (But Were Afraid to Ask Hitchcock)*. Ed. Slavoj Žižek. London: Verso, 1992. 125–28.

———. *Looking Awry: An Introduction to Jacques Lacan through Popular Culture*. Cambridge: MIT Press, 1991.

———. *The Sublime Object of Ideology*. London: Verso, 1989.

Zumthor, Paul. *Toward a Medieval Poetics*. Minneapolis: University of Minnesota Press, 1992.

Index

Abjection, 9
Arthur (King), 76
Arthurian Romance, 41, 103, 106

Basilisk, 2
Belakane, 68–70
Berger, John, 54
Brick enclosure, 42, 145
Bumke, Joachim, 12, 91
Burns, E. Jane, 94, 155n2, 155n4

Camilla, 38, 57–59
Carthage, 48, 50, 51, 57, 60
Chodorow, Nancy, 8, 20, 26, 82, 123
Clover, Carol, 38, 48, 123
Codex Manesse, 63
Conduct literature, 4, 9, 14, 21, 27, 30–33, 37, 47, 53
Condwiramurs, 82, 125
Courtly romance, 9, 30
Cundrie, 85, 86

Der Stricker, 4, 11, 18, 31, 33, 37, 39–46, 88, 123, 145
Der Welsche Gast, 11, 13, 14, 31, 32, 47, 98
Dido, 47, 48, 51–53, 55–57, 61, 68, 69, 106, 115, 154n5
Diegetic gaze, 38, 75, 105
Doppelweg, 85, 112
Doyenneship, 106
Dundes, Alan, 2, 3

Eneas, 4, 47, 48–62, 68, 69, 106
Eneasroman, 4, 47, 48, 53, 57, 68, 122
Enite, 83, 88, 91–96, 98–104, 115
Erec, 4, 31, 32, 51, 83, 85, 88–96, 98, 100–104, 115
Eurydice, 1, 56
Evil-eye, 1, 2

Fetish, 5, 7, 80
Freud, Sigmund, 4, 6–8, 113, 114, 116, 125
Friedrich von Hausen, 117

Gahmuret, 68–73
Gawain, 13, 19, 86, 111, 113, 115, 119, 120
Gender identity, 20, 82, 124
Gilbert, Dorothy, 103
Gottfried von Strassburg, 18, 34, 54, 98
Griselda, 100, 125
Guinevere, 18, 88, 89, 155n1
Guivreiz, 115
Gurnemanz, 79, 80, 82

Hades, 1, 56
Hartmann von Aue, 51, 88, 98, 105
Heinrich von Melk, 11, 35, 36, 40, 123, 127
Heinrich von Veldecke, 47, 62
Herzeloyde, 71–74, 82, 84, 115
Hildebrantslied, 50, 74
Hugo von Trimberg, 11, 27, 35, 36, 154n4
Huote, 17–20, 98

Irigaray, Luce, 6, 40
Isidor of Seville, 12, 20
Isolde, 18, 34, 47
Ither, 77, 79, 115
Iwein, 85, 105–7, 109–13, 116–19, 121, 156n3

Jaeger, Stephen, 121
Jeschute, 76, 100
Johnston, Claire, 5

Kalogrenant, 105
Kaplan, Ann, 56
Kelly, Kathleen Coyne, 75, 84
Key (Sir), 13, 14, 78, 79, 86

Lacan, Jacques, 91
Laqueur, Thomas, 75
Laudine, 19, 106, 107, 109, 111–13, 118, 119
Lavinia, 56, 59–62
Lunete, 106, 109, 111, 118, 119

Mabonagrin, 102
Mariolatry, 73, 99
Medusa, 1, 85, 153n1
Minne, 18, 51, 69, 71, 72, 77
Minnemonolog, 61
Minnesang, 153n2
Misogyny, 36, 45, 123
Morality tale, 4, 13
Mulvey, Laura, 4, 5, 113, 116

Newman, Barbara, 73, 100

Ordo, 4, 10, 18, 27, 36, 123
Oringles (Count of), 98, 110, 111
Orpheus, 1, 56

Parzival, 4, 32, 68, 73–87, 92, 100, 115, 122
Patriarchy, 3, 4, 6, 7, 26, 44, 45, 75, 122, 124
Pelrapeire, 81, 82
Phallus, 5
Psychoanalytic theory, 4, 8, 122

Rasmussen, Ann Marie, 23, 26

Saint Agnes, 99
Saint Augustine, 3, 34
Schultz, James, 38, 54, 84
Scopophilia, 5, 114, 124
Sedgwick, Eve Kosofsky, 75
Sexual gaze, 21, 47, 87, 114
Solterer, Helen, 53

Thomasin von Zerclaere, 3, 11, 13–17, 27, 30, 32, 36, 37, 98, 123
Tilak, 2
Tristan, 18, 34, 50, 54, 98
Troy, 50, 55
Troyes, Chrétien de, 89, 94, 103

Veiling (of women), 2
Venus, 51, 52, 54, 59, 60
Vikings, 50

Westphal, Sarah, 30, 37, 38
Winnicott, Donald, 7, 8, 123, 125
Winsbecke, Der, 21, 22, 37
Winsbeckin, Die, 4, 11, 21, 22, 25, 26, 36, 39
Witches, 3, 125, 155n1
Wolfram (von Eschenbach), 68

Sandra Lindemann Summers holds a PhD in German studies from Duke University. She currently teaches German at Elon University.

www.ingramcontent.com/pod-product-compliance
Lightning Source LLC
Chambersburg PA
CBHW021402090426
42742CB00009B/967